R. Gupta's®

Hand Book of

Computer Science

by:
P. KUMAR
B.Tech. (Computer Sc. & Engg.)
NIIT Jamshedpur (India)

RAMESH PUBLISHING HOUSE, NEW DELHI

Published by
O.P. Gupta *for* Ramesh Publishing House

Admin. Office
12-H, New Daryaganj Road, Opp. Officers' Mess,
New Delhi-110002 ✆ 23275224, 23245124

E-mail: info@rameshpublishinghouse.com
For Online Shopping: www.rameshpublishinghouse.com

Showroom
- Balaji Market, Nai Sarak, Delhi-6 ✆ 23253720, 23282525
- 4457, Nai Sarak, Delhi-6, ✆ 23918938

Book Code: R-1513

9th Edition: November 2024

ISBN: 978-93-5012-281-5

Price: ₹ 110

Printed at: Deepak Offset, Delhi

Hand Book of

COMPUTER SCIENCE

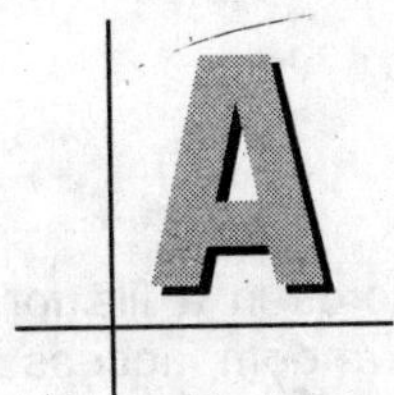

AAAS

This stands for American Association for the Advancement of Science.

Abnormal termination

Termination of a process by the operating system when the process could not continue. When a process reaches a successful conclusion it terminates normally. There are common scenario to inform the initiator of the process as termination was normal or abnormal.

Abort

Spontaneous fetal death of a process.

Abstraction

Ignoring those aspects of a subject that are not relevant to the current purpose. This is essential in the understanding of all forms of computer system.

Acceleration time

The time taken by device to reach its operating speed from the quiescent state.

Access control

The process by which access to resources of a computer system is limited or controlled.

Access matrix

This is two dimensional array.

Access method

This is a technique used for selecting records in a file for processing, retrieval or storage; like random access, sequential access etc.

Access time

The time taken to retrieve an item from memory.

Accumulator

A register that is used to contain the results of an operation performed by the arithmetic and logic unit. It can be one of the inputs to the ALU. In addition to holding results, the accumulator commonly has the ability to perform the various shift and circular shift instructions.

Ackermann's function

The function A defined inductively on pairs of non-negative integers in the following manner :

$$A(0, p) = p + 1$$
$$A(m + 1, 0) = A(m, 1)$$
$$A(m + 1, p + 1) = A(m, A(m + 1), p)$$

where $m, n \geq 0$, Thus

$$A(1, p) = p + 2$$
$$A(2, p) = 2p + 3$$

It is popular choice for testing the ability of compilers or computers to handle recursion.

This is also regarded as a function 'Ack' of a single variable:

$$\text{Ack}(p) = A(p, p)$$

Acoustic coupler

A type of modem that converts serial digital data into a frequency shift keyed sound signal in the audio range for transmission down telephone lines and decodes similar incoming sound signals.

Active star

A network topology in which the outer nodes connect to a single central node. The central node processes all messages in the network, including messages that it forwards from one outer node to another. A failure of the central node causes the entire network to fail.

Acyclic Graph

A graph possessing no cycles.

Adder

The "Adder" is a arithmetic component of digital computer. It is used for adding arithmetic digits. It takes input as binary number. The digits in the units's digit place in the addends are added first when decimal numbers are added digit by digit. But If the result is a two-digit number, only the digit in the units place of this number is entered in the unit's place of the sum; the tens are carried — that is, the digit in the ten's place is added to the digits in the ten's places of the original addends. The addition operation is then carried out on the ten's digits. Same process is continuously repeated for the higher order digits until the final sum is obtained. As an example, let us consider the addition of 151,67 & 8.The digits 1, 7 and 8 are added first. Since the result is the two-digit number 16, the 6 is entered in the unit's place of the final sum, and the 1 is carried. The sum of 1,5 and 6 is 12.The 2 is placed at ten's place of the final sum, and the 1 is carried. Since the sum of 1 and 1 is 2, the digit in the hundred place in the final sum is 2. The final sum is 226.

The circuit of Adder are:

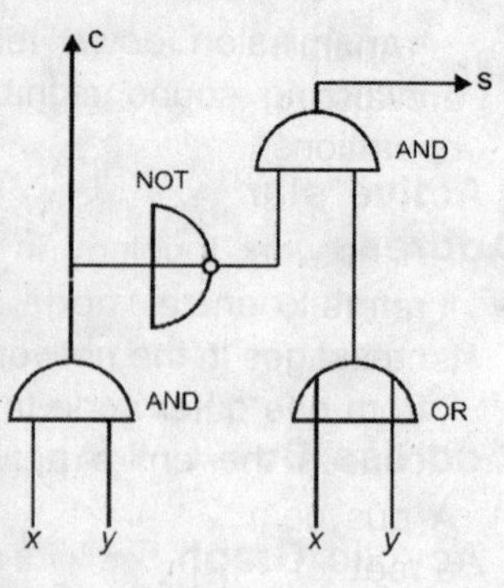

There are two types of Adder – Half and Full. A multi-digit adder for digit-by-digit addition usually consists of suitably connected single-digit adding units. The simplest such unit for the addition of binary numbers is called a half-adder. The circuit of a half-adder may vary in accordance with the system of logic elements used. The half-adder adds the two numbers *x* and *y* to produce the sum digit *S* and the carry digit *c* (see Table).

There are different circuit designs and combinations of elements used in adders. The various types of adders differ in the following ways: number system used, number of inputs (two-input and three-input), manner of handling multi-digit numbers (serial, parallel, and serial-parallel), of organizing the summation process (combinational and accumulating), and manner of organizing the carry circuits (sequential carry, ripple-through carry, group carry, and simultaneous carry). The type of adder chosen for a particular purpose depends primarily on the system of elements used in the computer and on the speed and economy requirements. Speed is one of the most important parameters of an adder. For the sake of speed in arithmetic operations, third-generation computers use not single-digit adders but group adders, which rapidly calculate the sums and carries for a group of digit places.

Inputs and Outputs of a Half-adder

Inputs		*Outputs*	
x	*y*	*S*	*c*
0	0	0	0
1	0	1	0
0	1	1	0
1	1	0	1

Apart from basic operation of addition, advanced adders are also used for multiplication, division, and various logical operations, such as logical addition and logical multiplication.

Address

It refers to location within memory of computer. This reference is used for accessing information.

Address Bus

A bus dedicated to passing address information. It may be a set of conducters that are physically seperated from other dedicated buses.

Address Comparator

Comparators are used for comparing two entities. The adjective "address" used with Comparator gives the specific meaning to the Comparator. It is used for the comparing address of two entities in computation for different purpose like identifying an entity.

Address Mapping

Converting address specified in an instruction into a machine address. Virtual memory and cache memory use forms of address mapping for additional memory managment function.

Address Register

A register which stores address.

Adjacency Matrix

A matrix used as a means of representing a graph. If *p* in the adjacency matrix corresponding to a given graph G, then

$$a_{ij} = 1$$

if there in an edge from vertex *i* to vertex *j* in G; otherwise

$$a_{ij} = 0$$

AI

Abbreviation of Artificial Intelligence.

Algebraic Language

A computer language whose statements are designed to resemble algebraic expressions.

Algol

Acronym for algorithmic language. The generic name of a high level language used in development of computing. The Association for Computing Machinery in the USA and Gessellschaft für, Angewante Mathematik and Mechanik in Europe set up a joint committee to define an international algorithmic language. This was known as Algol.

Algorithm

A prescribed set of well defined rules or instructions for the solution of a problem. Expressing an algorithm in a formal notation is one of the main parts of a programe.

Allocate

To assign a resource for use in performing a specific task. In computer communication, if any resource is allocated to particular process then it can not be used by other process till it is released by the previous one. If other may forcibly try to capture this, there arises the case of a dead lock.

Alphanumeric character

This is combination of alphabet (A – Z) and decimal digit (0 – 9).

ALU

Stands for Arithmetic and Logic Unit.

Alteration Gate

This is similar to OR gate. This is used for addition of data.

Ambiguity

This is the ability to express more than one interpretation. It is inherent error caused by multiple bit changes at code transition, position, which is eliminated by various scanning techniques.

AMC

This refers to Automatic Message Counting. Counters are used in counting the messages. This is most important technique in data communication based on packet.

AMD

This refers to Air Movement Data. Data presents most often with digital displays relating to flight-plan information, such as present position, future position etc.

ANSI

This stands for the ***A**merican **N**ational **S**tandards **I**nstitute* founded in 1918 and functions as voluntary organization. It creates standards for the computer industry. In addition to programming languages, ANSI sets standards for a wide range of technical areas, from electrical specifications to communications protocols. For example, ANSI C is a version of the C language that has been approved by the ANSI committee. To a large extent, all ANSI C compilers, regardless of which company produces them, should behave similarly.

For example, TCP/IP, the main set of protocols for sending data over fibre optic cables, is an ANSI standard.

AOP

This stands for Automatic Data Processing which is used to avoid manual processing of data in communication. Big computers like Super Computer are based on this principle.

Ambiguous Grammar

A context free grammar that derives the same word by different derivation trees e.g.,

$S \rightarrow$ if C then S else S

$S \rightarrow$ if C then S

Where S and C stand for statement and condition.

Amplifier

An Amplifier is a device which accepts an input signal and produces an output signal with stronger and larger amplitude that varies in the same way as the input. The input credential may be a current, a voltage, a mechanical motion, or any other signal. Electronic transistors or electron tubes as their principal components are the most common types of amplifiers. These are used in audio and stereo systems, intercoms, radio and television transmitters and receivers and other consumer electronic devices. In one type of single-transistor amplifier, known as a common-emitter circuit, a varying input voltage is fed to the base of the transistor, and the output appears at the transistor's collector; the ratio of the output voltage to the input voltage is called the voltage gain. For many purposes, a single transistor does not provide sufficient gain, or amplification. In a cascade, or multistage, amplifier, the output of the first amplifying device (transistor) is fed as input to the second amplifying device, whose output is fed as input to the third, and so on until an adequate signal amplification has been achieved. In a device such as a radio receiver, several amplifiers boost a weak input signal until it is powerful enough to drive a speaker. Usually, multi-stage amplifiers are not made of discrete components, but are built as integrated circuits. Another less common group of electronic amplifiers use magnetic devices as their principal components. There are also, many kinds of mechanical amplifiers, e.g., the power steering system of an automobile. See operational amplifier.

Amplitude Modulation

It refers to modulating the incoming waves with respect to amplitude. This is one of the principal methods of transmitting audio, video, or other types of information using radio waves, the relevant signal being superimposed onto a radio-frequency carrier wave. The frequency of the carrier wave remains unchanged but its amplitude is varied in accordance with the amplitude of the input signal.

AMR

It represents Automatic Message Registering. Used for notifying the messages without manual use.

Analog computer

A computer that performs computations by manipulating continuous physical variables that are analogs of the quantities being subjected to computation. The most commonly used physical variable is — voltage.

Analog signal

A signal that varies continuously in amplitude and time.

Analog-Digital Converter

This is a device to converting analog signal (current, voltage, or electric charge etc.) into digital signal. Digital signals are framed from digits '0' and '1'. An analog-to-digital converter (ADC) performs the reverse operation of Digital – Analog Converter (DAC). Signals are easily stored and transmitted in digital form, but a DAC is needed for the signal to be recognized by human senses or other non-digital systems.

A common use of analog-to digital converters is generation of digital signals from analog information in electronics devices. The quality of digital signals are more richer than analog. Today digital signals are preferred over analog signals.

Analyst

A person who defines a problem, determines exactly what is required in the solution, and defines the outlines of the machine solution. They are experts in automatic data processing applications.

Analyser

A person responsible for the checking of a program as well as analysing the requirements. Based on the requirements, they suggest the solution.

AND Gate

An electronic logic gate whose output is logic 1 (true) only when all inputs are logic 1, otherwise it is logic 0 (false)

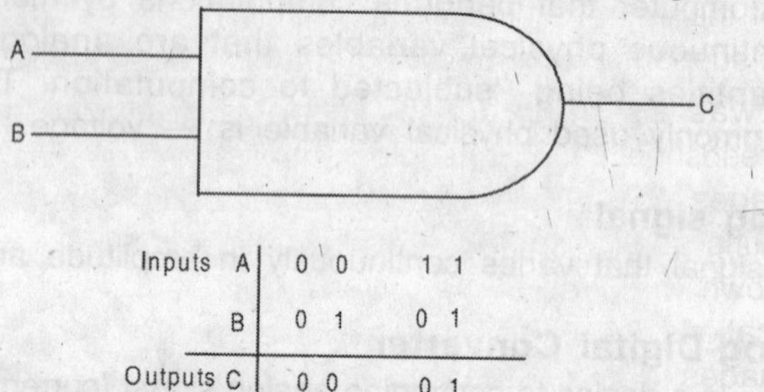

Antisymmetric Relation

A relation R defined on a set S and having the property that whenever x R y and y R x

then $x = y$

where x and y are arbitrary members of S.

APL

This is a Programming Language. It is based on Kenneth E. Iverson's mathematical notation which have special attributes for the design and specifications of digital computing systems, both hardware and software. It has a combination of uncommon and relatively unique features that appeal to programmers and make it a productive programming language.

The advantages of APL are:

- It is solution pointed, emphasizing the expression of algorithms independently of machine architecture or operating system.
- It is specific, using symbols rather than words and applying functions to entire arrays without using explicit loops.
- It has just one simple, consistent, and recursive precedence rule: the right argument of a function is the result of the entire expression to its right.
- It supports problem solving at a high level of abstraction.

It was an important influence on the development of spreadsheets, functional programming, and computer math packages. It is used in statistical, actuarial, financial, and scientific applications where it is used by practitioners for their own work and by programmers to develop commercial applications. It has also inspired several other programming languages. It is also associated with rapid and lightweight development projects in volatile business environments.

Application Layer

This is a layer of seven layer model.

Application Programme

Any programme that is specific to the particular role that a given computer performs within a given organisation and makes direct contribution to performing that role, e.g.; VLC media player, microsoft word etc.

Archived file

A file that has been transferred to a lower level in the memory hierarchy:

Argument

An argument is a special kind of **parameter**, used in a function to refer to one of the pieces of data provided as input to the function. Just as in standard mathematical usage, the *argument* is thus the actual value passed to a function, procedure, or routine (such as *x* in log *x*), whereas the *parameter* is a reference to that value inside the implementation of the function (log in this case).

Arithmetic Expression

Combination of arithmetic terms, arithmetic operators and paired parentheses. It uses 0 to 9 digits to frame the expression.

ARM

This stands for Automated Route Management. This is used in sending data in data-communication in a network.

ARPANET

This is a wide-area network created by the United States Defence Advanced Research Project Agency (ARPA) established in 1969. This was first packet switching network. It served for new networking technologies, linking many universities and research centers. UCLA and the Stanford Research Institute were the first two nodes that formed the ARPANET, followed shortly thereafter by the University of Utah.

ASCII

This stands for **American Standard Code for Information Interchange**. This is English alphabet based character-encoding scheme. ASCII codes support text in computers, communications equipment, and other devices that use text. Modern character-encoding schemes are based on ASCII and they support many more characters as well. The first commercial use of ASCII was as a seven-bit teleprinter code promoted by Bell data services. Work on ASCII formally began in 1960, with the first meeting of the American Standards Association's (ASA) X3.2 subcommittee. The first edition of the standard was published during 1963, a major revision during 1967, and the most recent update during 1986. Compared to earlier telegraph codes, the proposed Bell code and ASCII were both ordered for more convenient sorting (i.e., alphabetization) of lists and added features for devices other than teleprinters.

Assembler

It converts the high level language into low level language. A program that produces executable machine code from symbolic assembly language. A programming language that is a close approximation of the binary machine code; also called *assembly code*.

Assembly Language

This is a low-level programming language for computers. It is also applicable for microprocessors, microcontrollers, and other programmable devices. It is framed from binary digit '0' and '1' which is identified by machine. This representation is usually defined by the hardware manufacturer, and is based on mnemonics that symbolize processing steps, processor registers, memory locations, and other language features. So it is thus specific to a certain physical (or virtual) computer architecture.

A utility program called an *assembler* is used to translate high level language into the target computer's machine code. The assembler performs a more or less isomorphic translation (a one-to-one mapping) from mnemonic statements into machine instructions and data. This is in contrast with high-level languages, in which a single statement generally results in many machine instructions.

Many advanced assemblers offer additional mechanisms to facilitate program development, control the assembly process, and aid debugging. In particular, most modern assemblers include a macro facility (described below), and are called *macro-assemblers*.

Assertion

A Boolean formula whose value is claimed to be true.

Associate Memory

A data-storage device in which a location is identified by its informational content rather than by names, addresses, or relative positions, and from which the data may be retrieved. Also known as associative storage.

Asynchronous

A computer in which the performance of any operation starts as a result of a signal that the previous operation has been completed, rather than on a signal from a master clock.

It refers to events that are not synchronized, or coordinated, in time. The asynchronous operations as: The interval between transmitting D and E is not the same as between E and F. The ability to initiate a transmission at either end. The ability to store and forward messages. Starting the next operation before the current one is completed. This is in contrast with synchronous.

ATM

Generally it is known as automated teller machines — that allow an individual to withdraw cash from your bank or credit account by the help of plastic card. While in computer science, ATM stands for Asynchronous Transfer Mode — a networking technology that transfers data in packets or cells of a fixed size.

It uses 53-byte cells (5 bytes for the address header and 48 bytes for the data). These cells can be processed through an ATM switch fast enough to maintain data transfer speed of over 600 mbps. The technology was designed for the high-speed transmission of all forms of media from basic graphics to full-motion video. Because the cells are so small, ATM equipment can transmit large amounts of data over a single connection while ensuring that no single transmission takes up all the bandwidth. It also allows Internet Service Providers (ISPs) to assign limited bandwidth to each customer. While this may seem like a downside for the customer, it actually improves the efficiency of the ISP's Internet connection, causing the overall speed of the connection to be faster for everybody.

Augmentation

An operation which adds or joins one thing to another, so that the result shall be greater than the original thing.

Automata Theory

This is the study of abstract machines and the computational problems that can be solved using these machines. We can say in more appropriate way, abstract 'mathematical' machines or systems in place of abstract machines. These abstract machines are called automata. Automata comes from the Greek word meaning "self-acting". It makes a *transition* (or *jump*) to another state according to its *transition function* (which takes the current state and the recent symbol as its inputs) when the automaton sees a symbol of input. Automata theory is also closely related to formal language theory. An automaton is a finite representation of a formal language that may be an infinite set. Automata are often classified by the class of formal languages they are able to recognize. Automata play a major role in theory of computation, compiler design and parsing.

Auxiliary Storage

This is a storage device in addition to the main storage of a computer; for example, magnetic tape, disk, or magnetic drum. Also known as auxiliary memory. This is more reliable way of storing data because hard disk of computer may be corrupt due to several reasons. A high-speed memory that is in a large mainframe or supercomputer, is not directly addressable by the central processing unit, and is connected to the main memory by a high-speed data channel.

Auto CAD

It is an application software for computer-aided design (CAD) drafting in both 2D and 3D. It was first released in 1982. It is used to make designs of buildings, robots etc. on computer. AutoCAD was one of the first CAD programs to run on personal computers. It uses the graphical representation. Today, there are several other types of such tools available in market like CAM. It assist engineers and designers in a wide variety of industries to design and manufacture physical products ranging from buildings, bridges, roads, aircraft, ships and cars to digital cameras, mobile phones, TVs, cloths, and of course computers!

Avalanche Transistor

It is a bipolar junction transistor. It is designed for operation in the region of its collector-current/collector-to-emitter voltage characteristics beyond the collector to emitter breakdown voltage, called avalanche breakdown region. Operation in the avalanche breakdown region is called avalanche mode operation. This region is characterized by avalanche breakdown, a phenomenon similar to Townsend discharge for gases, and negative differential resistance. It gives avalanche transistors the ability to switch very high currents with less than a nano-second rise and fall times (transition times).

❑ ❑ ❑

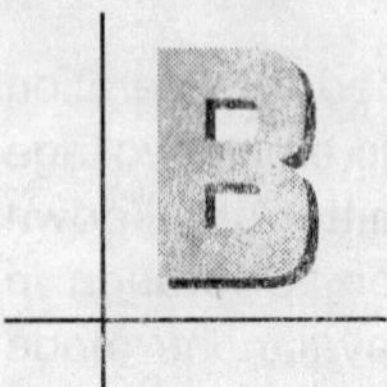

Back–End Processor

There are several layers between hardware, server and end user in software application.They are mostly known as front-end and back-end processor. Front-end is also known as User interface for interacting with back-end.

The model-view-controller in software design for example, provides front and back ends for the database, the user, and the data processing components. The separation of software systems into front and back ends simplifies development and separates maintenance.

For major computer subsystems, a graphical file manager is a front end to the computer's file system, and a shell interfaces the operating system — the front end faces the user and the back end launches the programs of the operating system in response.

Backtracking

This is an algorithm for finding solutions to computational problems, that incrementally builds candidates to the solutions, and abandons each partial candidate *c* ("backtracks") as soon as it determines that *c* cannot possibly be completed to a valid solution.

The example of the use of backtracking is the "eight queens puzzle", that asks for all arrangements of eight queens on a standard chessboard so that no queen attacks any other. In the common backtracking approach, the partial candidates are arrangements of *k* queens in the first *k* rows of the board, all in different rows and columns. Any partial solution that contains two mutually attacking queens can be abandoned, since it cannot possibly be completed to a valid solution.

This can be applied only for problems which admit the concept of a "partial candidate solution" and a relatively quick test of whether it can possibly be completed to a valid solution. Backtracking is an important tool for solving constraint satisfaction problems, such as crosswords, verbal arithmetic, Sudoku, and many other puzzles. It is often the most convenient (if not the most efficient technique for parsing, for the knapsack problem and other combinatorial optimization problems. It is also the basis of the so called logic programming languages such as Icon, Planner and Prolog. Backtracking is also utilized in the (diff) difference engine for the Media Wiki software.

Backtracking depends on user-given "black box procedures" that define the problem to be solved, the nature of the partial candidates, and how they are extended into complete candidates. It is therefore a metaheuristic rather than a specific algorithm — although, unlike many other meta-heuristics, it is guaranteed to find all solutions to a finite problem in a bounded amount of time.

Backup

A copy of a program or file that is stored separately from the original.This is helpful in retrieving data in case of data-loss or damage.

Band

A set of adjacent tracks on a magnetic disk. In data communication, it is known as range of frequencies.

Band limited channel

A transimission channel with finite bandwith. All physically realizable channels are band limited.

Band Matrix

This is a sparse matrix whose non-zero entries are confined to a diagonal *band*, comprising the main diagonal and zero or more diagonals on either side. A matrix is called a **band matrix** or **banded matrix** if its bandwidth is reasonably small. Working with band matrices is always preferential to working with similarly dimensioned square matrices.

Bandwith

This is range of frequency like, 200hz to 300hz. In computer networking and computer science, bandwidth, network bandwidth, data bandwidth, or digital bandwidth is a measure of available or consumed data communication resources expressed in bits/second or multiples of it (kilobits/s, megabits/s etc.).

On wireless communications, modem data transmission, digital communications, electronics, etc., bandwidth refers to analog signal bandwidth measured in hertz — the original meaning of the term. Few scholars represent it such as *bit rate*, *channel capacity* and *throughput* rather than bandwidth in bit/s, to avoid this confusion.

Bank Switching

This is a algorithm to enhance the amount of usable memory beyond the amount directly addressable by the processor. It can be used to configure a system differently at different times; for example, a ROM required to start a system from diskette could be switched off when no longer needed.

Many modern micro-controllers and micro-processors use bank switching to manage random-access memory, non-volatile memory, input-output devices and system management registers in small embedded systems. The technique was common in 1 byte microcomputer systems. It may also be used to work around limitations in address bus width, where some hardware constraint prevents straight-forward addition of more address lines. Unlike memory management by "paging", data is not exchanged with a mass storage device like disk memory. Data remains in quiescent storage in a memory area that is not currently accessible to the processor.

Bar Code

The machine-readable representation of the UPC. Bar codes are read by a scanner that passes over the code and registers the UPC. The width of each black line and the subsequent white space between each line coincides with the numbers of the UPC.

A series of vertical parallel bars of varying widths, in which each of the digits zero through nine are represented by a different pattern of bars that can be read by a laser scanner. The bars are commonly found on consumer products and are used especially for inventory control.

Batch Processing

A bunch of data are processed as a unit without any manual intervention is known as Batch processing.That is why all input data is pre-selected through scripts or command-line parameters. This is in contrast to "online" or interactive programs which prompt the user for such input. A program takes a set of data files as input, processes the data, and produces a set of output data files. This operating environment is termed as "batch processing" because the input data are collected into batches of files and are processed in batches by the program.

Baud Rate

The *baud*, therefore, indicates the number of bits per second that are transmitted. Baud Rate is the number of *signaling elements* that occur each second. The term is named after J.M.E. Baudot, the inventor of the Baudot telegraph code.

Only one bit of information is encoded in each electrical change at slow speeds. For example, *300 baud* means that 300 bits are transmitted each second (abbreviated *300 bps*). Assuming asynchronous communication, which requires 10 bits per character, this translates to 30 characters per second (cps). For slow rates (below 1,200 baud), you can divide the baud by 10 to see how many characters per second are sent.

At higher speeds, it is possible to encode more than one bit in each electrical change. 4,800 baud may allow 9,600 bits to be sent each second. At high data transfer speeds, therefore, data transmission rates are usually expressed in bits per second (bps) rather than baud. For example, a 9,600 bps modem may operate at only 2,400 baud.

BCD adder

This is 4 bit binary adder that is capable of adding two 4 bit words having BCD (binary coded decimal) format.

Biconditional

A logical statement combining two statements, truth values in such a way that the outcome is true only if both are true or both are false. If any one became false or true then it fails.

Biconnected Graph

Any graph connected from both sides like A → B and B ← A. A graph G, either directed or undirected with the property that for every three distinct vertices u, v and w there is a path from u to w not contaning v. For an undirected graph, this is equivalent to the graph having no cut vertes.

Bijection

This is one-to-one onto function. A function that is both injection and a surjection. Every element of parent have only one relation with child in mapping of function.

Binary Code

This is also known as Base Two code. It has two values 0 and 1 representing OFF and ON respectively. Computers use Base Two because all of the work is done by transistors; tiny switches etc. The switches can either be OFF (0) or ON (1). Check out the power switch on your appliances at home. Many of them will show 0 and 1 (off and on). Learning Base Two is easy and fun. In order to proceed, you must first understand how number systems work.

Binary Search Tree

A binary search tree (BST), also called a **sorted binary tree** or **ordered tree. This** is a node-based binary tree data structure which has the following properties:

- The left subtree of a node contains only nodes with keys less than the node's key.
- The right subtree of a node contains only nodes with keys greater than the node's key.
- Both the left and right subtrees must also be binary search trees.

Generally, the information represented by each node is a record rather than a single data element. However, for sequencing purposes, nodes are compared according to their keys rather than any part of their associated records.

The advantage of binary search trees over other data structures is that the related sorting algorithms and search algorithms such as in-order traversal can be very efficient.

Binary search trees are a fundamental data structure used to construct more abstract data structures such as sets, multisets, and associative arrays.

Binary System

This is a data structure in which each node has at most two child nodes, distinguished as "left" and "right" child node. Nodes with children are parent nodes, and child nodes may contain references to their parents. Outside the tree, there is often a reference to the "root" node (the ancestor of all nodes), if it exists. Any node in the data structure can be reached by starting at root node and repeatedly following references to either the left or right child. This is used to implement binary search trees and binary heaps.

Bipolar Signal

A signal whose signaling elements consist of both positive and negative voltages. Bipolar signals are used in data-communication systems.

Biquinary Code

This is a numeral encoding scheme practised in many abacuses and in some early computers, including the Colossus. The term "*bi-quinary*" indicates that the code comprises both a two-state (*bi*) and a five-state (*quinary*) component. The encoding resembles that used by many abacuses, with four beads indicating either 0.4 or 5..9 and another bead indicating which of those ranges.

Bit

Represents short of ***bi**nary digi**t***, the smallest unit of information on a machine. The term was first used in 1946 by

John Tukey, a leading statistician and adviser to five presidents. This can hold only one digit '0' or '1'. More meaningful information is obtained by combining consecutive bits into larger units. For example, a byte is composed of 8 consecutive bits.

Bit Mapping

A set of bits that represents a graphic image, with each bit or group of bits corresponding to a pixel in the image.

Bit Rate

The rate of flow of binary digits in a digital data-processing system.This is usually expressed as the number of bits per second. The speed of any network is identified by this.

Bit Stuffing

The insertion of extra bits in a transmission of data in order to fill a frame to a fixed size or to break up a pattern of bits that could be mistaken for control codes.This distinguished between two messages or packets.The practice of adding bits to a stream of data. Bit stuffing is required by many network and communications protocols for the following reasons:

- To prevent *data* being interpreted as *control* information. For example, many frame-based protocols, such as X.25, signal the beginning and end of a frame with six consecutive 1 bits.
- Therefore, if the actual data being transmitted has six 1 bits in a row, a zero is inserted after the first 5 so that the data is not interpreted as a frame delimiter. Of course, on the receiving end, the stuffed bits must be discarded.
- For protocols that require a fixed-size frame, bits are sometimes inserted to make the frame size equal to this set size.
- For protocols that require a continuous stream of data, zero bits are sometimes inserted to ensure that the stream is not broken.

BNF

Backus–Naur Form (BNF) is used to express context-free grammars. This is a way to describe formal languages developed by John Backus and Peter Naur by using two sets of rules; i.e., lexical rules and syntactic rules. BNF is widely used as a notation for the grammars of computer programming languages, instruction sets and communication protocols, as well as a notation for representing parts of natural language grammars. Many textbooks for programming language theory and/or semantics document the programming language in BNF.

There are various extensions and types of BNF, including Extended and Augmented Backus–Naur Forms (EBNF and ABNF).

Boolean Function

Assembled by the application of the operations AND, OR, NOT on the variables *x, y,..., z* and elements whose common domain is a Boolean algebra.

Bottom-up Parsing

This is a type of Parsing, strategy for frame information that attempts to identify the most fundamental units first, and then to infer higher-order structures from them. The name comes from the concept of a parse tree, in which the most fundamental units are at the bottom, and structures composed of them are in successively higher layers, until at the top of the tree a single unit, or *start symbol*, comprises all of the information being analyzed. Bottom-up parsing occurs in the analysis of both natural languages and computer languages. It is contrasted with top-down parsing, in which complex units are divided into simpler parts until all of the information is parsed.

Breadbord

This is a construction base for prototyping of electronics. This is also known as "Plugboard" and "Solderless Board".

Solderless breadboard does not require soldering, it is reusable. This makes it easy to use for creating temporary prototypes and experimenting with circuit design. Older breadboard types did not have this property. A stripboard (veroboard) and similar prototyping printed circuit boards, which are used to build permanent soldered prototypes or one-offs, cannot easily be reused. A variety of electronic systems may be prototyped by using breadboards, from small analog and digital circuits to complete central processing units (CPUs).

Breadth-first Search

This is way of searching the graph starting from root node and explores all existing nodes in graph. Then for each of those nearest nodes, it explores their unexplored neighbor nodes, and so on, until it finds the goal.

Browser

A program that accesses and displays files and other data available on the Internet and other networks. Users send requests to server with the help of Browser; .e.g. Mozila firefox, internet explore, google chrome.

Bubble Sort

This is an algorithm to sort the data. This is also known as "sinking sort", works by repeatedly stepping through the list to be sorted, comparing each pair of adjacent items and swapping them if they are in the wrong order. The pass through the list is repeated until no swaps are needed, which indicates that the list is sorted. The algorithm gets its name from the way smaller elements "bubble" to the top of the list. Because it only uses comparisons to operate on elements, it is a comparison sort. Although the algorithm is simple, it is not efficient for sorting large lists; other algorithms are better.

Bucket Sort

This is a technique of sorting the data. It is also known as "Bin Sort." It is a sorting algorithm that works by partitioning an array into a number of buckets. Each bucket is then sorted individually, either using a different sorting algorithm, or by recursively applying the bucket sorting algorithm. It is a distribution sort, and is a cousin of radix sort in the most to least significant digit flavour. Bucket sort is a generalization of pigeon-hole sort. Since bucket sort is not a comparison sort, the O ($n \log n$) lower bound is inapplicable. The computational complexity estimates involve the number of buckets.

Buddy System

The utilization of space and the running speed of the buddy system are considered. Equations are derived that give various statistical properties of the buddy system. For the bottom level with Poisson requests and exponential service times the expected amount of space wasted by pairing full cells with empty cells is about 0.513 &rgr;1/2 and the mean time between requests from the bottom level to the next level is about 1.880 & rgr; 1/2 & lgr; –1, where & rgr; is the mean number of blocks in use on the bottom level and &lgr; –1 is the mean time between requests for blocks on the bottom level. The results of a number of simulations of the buddy system are also given and compared with the analytical studies.

Buffering

A method used to store data temporarily. It is helpful in data communication specially when speed of incoming data varied from outgoing data and vice-versa.

Bug

An error in program or system. This is also identified as unwanted result. It is necessary to identified bug in software programme to run it successfully.

referred to as lazy evaluation as only those pages demanded by the process are swapped from secondary storage to main memory. When a process is to be swapped into main memory for processing, the pager guesses which pages will be used prior to the process being swapped out again. The pager will only load these pages into memory. This process avoids loading pages that are unlikely to be used and focuses on pages needed during the current process execution period. Therefore, not only is unnecessary page load during swapping avoided but we also try to pre-empt which pages will be needed and avoid loading pages during execution.

de Morgan's Law

This is rule relating the logical operators "and" and "or" in terms of each other via negation. With two operands A and B. This is notified as

$$\overline{A \cdot B} = \overline{A} + \overline{B}$$

$$\overline{A + B} = \overline{A} \cdot \overline{B}$$

We can also write it as

NOT (A OR B) = (NOT A) AND (NOT B)

NOT (A AND B) = (NOT A) OR (NOT B)

Demultiplexer

It decodes the signal sent by Multiplexer by taking one data input from a number of selection inputs, and convert them into multiple one as it was as at the time of input to multiplexer. They forward the data input to one of the outputs depending on the values of the selection inputs. Demultiplexers are sometimes convenient for designing general purpose logic, because if the demultiplexer's input is always true. It acts as a decoder. The Multiplexer and Demultiplexer are always used in pair.

Bus Topology

This is a topology to connect different machines to each other. It is preferred in local area network. In this each computer or server is connected to the single bus cable. A signal from the source travels in both directions to all machines connected on the bus cable until it finds the intended recipient. If the machine address does not match the intended address for the data, the machine ignores the data. Alternatively, if the data matches the machine address, the data is accepted. It is inexpensive to implement compared to other topologies beacuse it uses only one wire. However, the low cost of implementing the technology is offset by the high cost of managing the network. Additionally, since only one cable is utilized, it can be the single point of failure. If the network cable is terminated on both ends and when without termination data transfer stops and when cable breaks, the entire network will be down.

Baseband

This refers to unaltered signals which are neither modulated nor converted to any form of signal. It is an adjective that describes signals and systems whose range of frequencies is measured from close to 0 hertz to a cut-off frequency, a maximum bandwidth or highest signal frequency; it is sometimes used as a noun for a band of frequencies starting close to zero. Baseband can often be considered as a synonym to "lowpass" or "non-modulated", and antonym to passband, bandpass, carrier-modulated or radio frequency (RF) signal.

Biconditional Gate

This is Exclusive NOR Gate. It is equivalent to Exclusive NAND and OR gate.

Billi

A specific prefix that designates the quantity one billion.

Binary Coded Decimal System

BCD (binary coded decimal) numbers representation are used in computers. With the 4-bits space you can address 16 numbers. But in BCD number system you only address 10 (0-9) numbers.

Biometric

This is a use of biological parts such as eye, voice, fingerprints etc. in recognising any individual. This is more authentic way of recognising someone. In computer science, in particular, biometrics is used as a form of identity access management and access control. It is also used to identify individuals in groups that are under surveillance. Biometric identifiers are the distinctive, measurable characteristics used to identify individuals. The two categories of biometric identifiers include physiological and behavioural characteristics. Physiological characteristics are related to the shape of the body, and include but are not limited to — fingerprint, face recognition, DNA, palm print, hand geometry, iris recognition (which has largely replaced retina), and odour/scent. Behavioural characteristics are related to the behavior of a person, including but not limited to — typing rhythm, gait, and voice. Some researchers have coined the term — behaviometrics to describe the latter class of biometrics.

More traditional means of access control include token-based identification systems, such as a driver's license or passport, and knowledge-based identification systems, such as a password or personal identification number. Since biometric identifiers are unique to individuals, they are more reliable in verifying identity than token and knowledge-based methods, however, the collection of biometric identifiers raises privacy concerns about the ultimate use of this information. This is mostly used for security purposes.

Boolean Add

Same as OR Gate. It is used in adding two binary digits.

Bootstrap Loader

This is the process of starting any computer when switched on. It loads necessary information before computer should function. The bootstrap loader is a small program that runs before any other normal program can run. It is stored on non-volatile storage (normally the computer's ROM) so that it can still be used after the computer has been switched-off and then switched on again. It gives instructions as to where the operating system, on a microcomputer, is to be found.

BOS/360

Basic Operating System/360.

Branching

This refers to dividing any sequence. This is a computer operation similar to switching, where selection is made between two or more possible courses of action. It is used in preparing flow chart.

Broadband

Broadband is the short form of Broadband Internet Access. It is a term describing a service that provides a connection to the Internet. It is normally more than 1.5 to 2 Mbit/s as identified in 1988 by CCITT. Today almost all networking sites are roaming on broadband. The US National Information Infrastructure project, during the 1990s, brought the term into public policy debates. Broadband became a marketing buzzword for telephone and cable companies to sell their more expensive higher data rate products, especially for Internet access. In the US National Broadband Plan of 2009, it was defined as "Internet access that is always on and faster than the traditional dial-up access". The same agency has defined it differently through the years. Even though information signals generally travel nearly the speed of light in the medium, no matter what the bit rate, higher rate services are often marketed as "faster" or "higher speeds". (This use of the word "speed" may or may not be appropriate, depending on context. It would be accurate, for instance, to say that a file of a given size will typically take less time to finish transferring if it is being transmitted via broadband as opposed to dial-up). Consumers are also targeted by advertisements for peak transmission rates, while actual end-to-end rates observed in practice can be lower due to other factors.

Buffer

This is an area of a physical memory storage used to temporarily hold data during communication. Typically, the data is stored in a buffer as it is retrieved from an input device or just before it is sent to output device such as printer. However, a buffer may be used when moving data between processes within a computer. This is comparable to buffers in telecommunication. Buffers can be implemented in a fixed memory location in hardware or by using a virtual data buffer in software, pointing at a location in the physical memory. In all cases, the data stored in a data buffer are stored on a physical storage media. A majority of buffers are implemented in software, which typically use the faster RAM to store temporary data, due to the much faster access time compared with hard disk drives. Buffers are typically used when there is a difference between the rate at which data is received and the rate at which it can be processed, or in the case that these rates are variable, for example -- in a printer spooler or in online video streaming.

and the entries specify whether (or in what order) the action is to be performed for the set of condition alternatives the entry corresponds to.

Many decision tables include in their condition alternatives the don't care symbol, a hyphen. Using don't cares can simplify decision tables, especially when a given condition has little influence on the actions to be performed. In some cases, entire conditions thought to be important initially are found to be irrelevant when none of the conditions influence which actions are performed.

Aside from the basic four quadrant structure, decision tables vary widely in the way the condition alternatives and action entries are represented. Some decision tables use simple true/false values to represent the alternatives to a condition, other tables may use numbered alternatives, and some tables even use fuzzy logic or probabilistic representations for condition alternatives. In a similar way, action entries can simply represent whether an action is to be performed, or in more advanced decision tables, the sequencing of actions to perform.

Demand Paging

This is opposed to Anticipatory Paging. This is an application part of virtual memory. The system which uses demand paging, the operating system copies a disk page into physical memory. If particular page did not found in memory then it is known as Page Fault.

It follows that a process begins execution with none of its pages in physical memory, and many page faults will occur until most of a process's working set of pages is located in physical memory. This is an example of lazy loading techniques.

It follows that pages which should only be brought into memory if the executing process demands them. This is often

BIOS

Basic input/output System.

Black box

This is a way of testing without knowing the contents of a programme. The opposite of this is "White Box".

In science and engineering, a black box is a device, system or object which can be viewed solely in terms of its input, output and transfer characteristics without any knowledge of its internal workings, that is, its implementation is "opaque" (black). Almost anything might be referred to as a black box—a transistor, an algorithm, or the human mind.

The opposite of a black box is a system where the inner components or logic are available for inspection, which is sometimes known as a white box, a glass box, or a clear box.

BMP

This is extension in which bit mapped graphic file ... contains a file generated using program such as PC paintbrush.

Bookmark

Storing the specific link address on a local machine. To mark a document or a specific place in a document for later retrieval. Nearly all Web browsers support a bookmarking feature that lets you save the address (URL) of a Web page so that you can easily re-visit the page at a later time.

Disjunction

This is also known as Inclusive Disjunction or Alternation. Its results are true whenever *one or more* of its operands are true. E.g. in this context, "*C* or D" is true if *C* is true, or if D is true, or if both C and D are true. In grammar, **or** is a coordinating conjunction.

In ordinary language, i.e. outside of contexts such as formal logic, mathematics and programming, "or" sometimes has the meaning of exclusive disjunction. E.g. "Please call me or send an email" means "do one or the other, but not both". On the other hand, "Her marks are so good that she's either very bright or studies hard" allows for the possibility that the person is both bright and works hard. In other words, in ordinary language "or" can mean inclusive or exclusive or. Usually it is clear from the context which is the intended meaning.

Distributed Database

This is a database in which storage devices are not all attached to a common CPU. It may be stored in several stations located in the same physical location, or may be dispersed over a network of interconnected computers.

A database can be distributed across multiple physical locations. It can reside on a network server on the Internet or on corporate intranets/extranets, or on other company networks. The replication and distribution of databases improves database performance at end-user worksites.

There are two processes — replication and duplication to assure the effectiveness of database. Replication involves using specialized software that looks for changes in the distributive database. Once the changes have been identified, the replication process makes all the databases look the same. The replication process can be very complex and time-consuming depending on the size and number of the

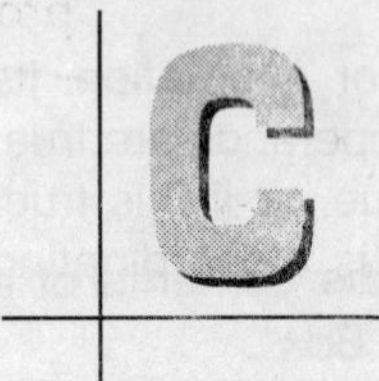

Cache Memory

It stores the data in temporary fashion. It keeps all frequently used data while operating the computer. It is handled by the operating system. It helps in saving the searching time because it will take more time for the operating system searching the data from secondary memory like hard disk.

Whenever operating system searches any data; it first look in the Cache memory. The data stored within a cache might be computed earlier or duplicates of original values that are stored elsewhere. If requested data is found in the cache then it is known as cache-hit. This request can be served by simply reading the cache, which is comparatively faster. While cache-miss is not-finding data in the cache. In that case the data has to be recomputed or fetched from its original storage location, which is comparatively slower. Hence, the greater the number of requests that can be served from the cache, the faster the overall system performance becomes.

To be cost efficient and to enable an efficient use of data, caches are relatively small. Nevertheless, caches have proven themselves in many areas of computing because access patterns in typical computer applications have locality of reference. References exhibit temporal locality if data is requested again that has been recently requested. References exhibit spatial locality if data is requested that is physically stored close to data that has been requested recently.

CAD

It is an application software for computer-aided design (CAD) drafting in both 2D and 3D. It was first released in 1982. It is used to make designs of building, robots etc. on computer. AutoCAD was one of the first CAD programs to run on personal computers. It uses the graphical representation. Today there are several other types of such tools available in market like CAM. It assist engineers and designers in a wide variety of industries to design and manufacture physical products ranging from buildings, bridges, roads, aircrafts, ships and cars to digital cameras, mobile phones, TVs, cloths and of course computers!

Card Reader

This is a data input device that reads data from a card-shaped storage medium. Historically, paper or cardboard punched cards were used throughout the initial several decades of the computer industry to store information and programs for computer system, and were read by punched card readers. More modern card readers are electronic devices that use plastic cards imprinted with barcodes, magnetic strips, computer chips or other storage medium.

A **memory card reader** is a device used for communication with a smart card or a memory card. A **magnetic card reader** is a device used to read magnetic strip cards, such as credit cards. A **business card reader** is a device used to scan and electronically save printed business cards.

Carrier System

A method of deriving two or more simultaneous continuous channels over a medium connecting two points by assigning separate portion of the bandwidth to the individual channel.

Cartridge

This is used in printer to store different colour. It is a reusable component. In general practice it is a cylindrical, usually metal casing containing the primer and charge of ammunition for firearms.

CGI

This stands for Computer Graphics Interface. The term computer graphics has been used in a broad sense to describe almost everything on computers that is not text or sound. Generally, it refers to several different things:

- the various technologies used to create and manipulate images
- the representation and manipulation of image data by a computer
- the images so produced, and
- the sub-field of computer science which studies methods for digitally synthesizing and manipulating visual content.

The examples of CGI are Computer imagery found on television, in newspapers, in weather reports, or in all kinds of medical investigation and surgical procedures. A well-constructed graph can present complex statistics in a form that is easier to understand and interpret. In the media "such graphs are used to illustrate papers, reports, thesis", and other presentation material.

There are several powerful tools which have been developed to visualize data. Computer generated imagery can be categorized into several different types — 2D, 3D, and animated graphics. As technology has improved, 3D computer graphics have become more common, but 2D computer graphics are still widely used. Over the past decade, other specialized fields have been developed like information visualization, and scientific visualization is more concerned with "the visualization of three dimensional phenomena (architectural, meteorological, medical, biological, etc.), where the emphasis is on realistic renderings of volumes, surfaces, illumination sources, and so forth, perhaps with a dynamic (time) component".

time, whereas membership in a deterministic context-free language can be tested in O(*n*) time, where n is the length of the string.

The deterministic context-free languages are exactly those recognized by some LR grammar.

Digital Computer

This is a computer that stores data in terms of binary numbers and proceeds in discrete steps from one state to the next. In digital computers, even letters, words and whole texts are represented digitally. Unlike analog computer, digital computers can only approximate a continuum by assigning large numbers of digits to a state description and by proceeding in arbitrarily small steps. The performance of digital computer are better than analog computer.

Diode

This is a type of two-terminal electronic device with *non-linear* conductance. This characteristic distinguishing it from components such as two-terminal linear resistors which obey Ohm's law. The most common function of a diode is to allow an electric current to pass in one direction (called the diode's *forward* direction), while blocking current in the opposite direction (the *reverse* direction). Thus, the diode can be thought of as an electronic version of a check valve. This unidirectional behaviour is called rectification, and is used to convert alternating current to direct current, and to extract modulation from radio signals in radio receivers — these diodes are forms of rectifiers.

There are several types of diodes. A semiconductor diode, the most common type today, is a crystalline piece of semiconductor material connected to two electrical terminals. A vacuum tube diode is a vacuum tube with two electrodes: a plate and a cathode.

Character Encoding

A binary encoding of given character set e.g., ASCII and EBCDIC. Encoding is a technique to convert one form of data into other.

Chip

This is an electronics circuit framed with the help of transistors, resistors, ICs etc. on a single board. We can also say, it is the shaped and processed semiconductor die that is mounted on a substrate to form a transistor, diode, or other semiconductor device. An integrated circuit performing a significant number of functions and constituting a subsystem. Also known as microchip.

Clock

Electronic pulses which are emitted periodically, usually by a crystal device, to synchronize the operation of circuits in a computer. Also known as clock signals.

Cluster

This is the latest technology in computer networking. A **computer cluster** is a group of linked computers, working together closely thus in many respects forming a single computer. The associates of a cluster are not always connected to each other through fast local area networks or other means. Clusters are usually deployed to improve performance and availability over that of a single computer, while typically being much more cost-effective than single computers of comparable speed or availability.

CMOS

This stands for ***C**omplementary **M**etal **M**ixed **S**emiconductor*. It is a widely used type of semiconductor in developing electronics circuit. CMOS semiconductors use both NMOS

a singly linked list, the operations are simpler and potentially more efficient (for nodes other than first nodes) because there is no need to keep track of the previous node during traversal or no need to traverse the list to find the previous node, so that its link can be modified.

DTL

This stands for Diode–transistor logic. It is framed through diodes and transistors. It is a class of digital circuits that is the direct ancestor of the transistor–transistor logic. It is called so because the logic gating function (e.g., AND) is performed by a diode network and the amplifying function is performed by a transistor (contrast this with RTL and TTL).

D-Flip-flop

This is the most common flip-flop in use. It is also known as *data* or *delay* flip-flop because its output Q looks like a delay of input D. The Q output takes on the state of the D input at the moment of a positive edge at the clock pin (or negative edge if the clock input is active low).

It is called the D flip-flop for this reason, since the output takes the value of the D input or *data* input, and *delays* it by one clock cycle. The D flip-flop can be interpreted as a primitive memory cell, zero-order hold, or delay line. Whenever the clock pulses, the value of Q_{next} is D and Q_{prev} otherwise. Where 'X' denotes a *Don't care* condition.

TRUTH TABLE OF D-FLIP-FLOP

Clock	*D*	*Q*	Q_{prev}
Rising edge	0	0	X
Rising edge	1	1	X
Non-Rising	X	Q_{prev}	

(negative polarity) and PMOS (positive polarity) circuits. They consume less power than chips using just one type of transistor due to the reason that only one of the circuit types is on at any given time. This makes them particularly attractive for use in battery-powered devices, such as portable computers. Personal computers also contain a small amount of battery-powered CMOS memory to hold the date, time, and system setup parameters.

CNF

This stands for **Conjunctive Normal Norm (CNF).** It is useful in automated theorem proving and similar to the product of sums form used in circuit theory. CNF have all conjunctions of literals and all disjunctions of literals, as they can be seen as conjunctions of one-literal clauses and conjunctions of a single clause, respectively. As in the disjunctive normal form (DNF), the only propositional connectives a formula in CNF can contain are "and", "or", and "not". The not operator can only be used as part of a literal, which means that it can only precede a propositional variable.

The example of formula in CNF are: $A \wedge B$

This is in CNF because it can be seen as the conjunction of the two single-literal clauses *A* and *B*. Incidentally, this formula is also in disjunctive normal form.

$A \vee B$

$(A \vee B) \wedge (\neg B \vee C \vee \neg D) \wedge (D \vee \neg E)$

The example of formula not in CNF are:

$(A \wedge B) \vee C$

$A \wedge (B \vee (D \wedge E))$.

COBOL

This is one of the oldest programming languages and stands for **Co**mmon **B**usiness-**O**riented **L**anguage, because of its primary domain in business, finance, and administrative systems for companies and governments. Even today big applications use COBOL due to its capability of handling like space technology, weather forecast etc. The COBOL 2002 standard includes support for object-oriented programming and other modern language features.

Code

A frame of combination of digits, letters or symbols, and rules for their association by means of which information can be represented or communicated for reasons of secrecy, brevity, etc. binary code method. There are different types of codes. But mainly it is high-level codes and low level codes. High level codes are framed by Programmer while low level codes are framed by compiler or interpreter. Low level code is also known as machine code framed in 0 and 1.

Column Vector

A type of matrix having one column. It means, it had only one column:

$$\begin{bmatrix} 1 \\ 2 \\ 3 \end{bmatrix}$$

Compaction

A technique for reducing the space required for data storage without losing any information content. This is also known as squishing. This is useful in sending data from one location to other because it reduces the space taken by original data. There are several tools used for compaction like WinZip, Rar, War etc.

Compilation Time

It is time taken by the Compiler or Interpreter to convert high level language into low level language, which will be understood by the machine. The machine languages are framed in binary digits. During compiling time compiler goes through several offering a graphical user interface (GUI), in particular by various Generations of the Microsoft Windows operating system.

Microsoft quickly bought the rights to QDOS (Quick and Dirty Operating System), also known as 86-DOS, from Seattle Computer Products, and began work on modifying it to meet IBM's specification. The first edition, MS-DOS 1.0, was launched in 1982. The version shipped with IBM's PCs was called PC DOS. Although MS-DOS and PC-DOS were initially developed in parallel by Microsoft and IBM, the two products eventually went their separate ways.

Ultimately it was the key product in Microsoft's growth from a programming languages company to a diverse software development firm, providing the company with essential revenue and marketing resources. It was also the underlying basic operating system on which early versions of Windows ran as a GUI.

Double Link List

This is a linked data structure that consists of a set of sequentially linked records called nodes. Each node contains two fields, called *links*, that are references to the previous and to the next node in the sequence of nodes. The beginning and ending nodes' **previous** and **next** links, respectively, point to some kind of terminator, typically a sentinel node or null, to facilitate traversal of the list. If there is only one sentinel node, then the list is circularly linked via the sentinel node. It can be conceptualized as two singly linked lists formed from the same data items, but in opposite sequential orders. Pictorially it can be seen as:

☒	•	12	•	•	99	•	•	37	•	☒

The two node links allow traversal of the list in either direction. While adding or removing a node in a doubly linked list requires changing more links than the same operations

processes like lexical analysis, semantic analysis etc. Compile time occurs before link time (when the output of one or more compiled files are joined together) and runtime (when a program is executed). It can also [illegible] the time required for compilation.

The operations performed at compile time generally includes syntax analysis, various kinds of semantic analysis (e.g., type checks and instantiation of template) and code generation.

Programming language definitions usually specify compile-time requirements that source code must meet to be successfully compiled. For example, the amount of storage required by types and variable can be deduced.

Properties of a program that can be reasoned about at compile time include range-checks (e.g., proving that an array index will not exceed the array bound), deadlock freedom in concurrent languages, or timings (e.g., proving that a sequence of code takes no more than an allocated amount of time).

In some programming languages, it may be necessary for some compilation and linking to occur at runtime. There is a trade-off between compile-time and link-time in that many compile-time operations can be deferred to link-time without incurring extra run-time.

Compiler

A compiler is a software or set of programs which transforms programming language known as source code into another computer language known as *target language*. The target languages are often having a binary form known as *object code*. The reason for transforming source code into target code is to create an executable program [illegible] by machine. The Compilers are specific to a programming language like Java Compiler, C Compiler etc.

A compiler is likely to perform many or all of the following operations: lexical analysis, pre-processing, parsing, semantic analysis (Syntax-directed translation), code generation, and optimization. These are specific to particular work.

It is primarily used for translate source code from a high level programming language to a lower level language (e.g., assembly language or machine code). If the compiled program can run on a computer whose CPU or operating system is different from the one on which the compiler runs, the compiler is known as a cross-compiler. A program that translates from a low level language to a higher level one is a *decompiler*. A program that translates between high-level languages is usually called a *language translator*, *source to source translator*, or *language converter*. A *language rewriter* is usually a program that translates the form of expressions without a change of language.

Program faults caused by incorrect compiler behaviour can be very difficult to track down and work around; therefore, compiler implementers invest a lot of time ensuring the correctness of their software.

DRAM

It stands for Dynamic random-access memory. It is a type of random-access memory that stores each bit of data in a separate capacitor within an integrated circuit. The capacitor can be either charged or discharged; these two states are taken to represent the two values of a bit, conventionally called 0 and 1. Since capacitors leak charge, the information eventually fades unless the capacitor charge is refreshed periodically. Because of this refresh requirement, it is a *dynamic* memory as opposed to SRAM and other *static* memory.

Computer

Modern computers are digital machines designed to sequentially and automatically carry out a sequence of arithmetic or logical operations. It is used for fast calculation of any requirement. It also facilitates multiple application symultaneously. The particular sequence of operations can be changed readily, allowing the computer to solve more than one kind of problem.

An important class of computer operations on some computing platforms is the accepting of input from human operators and the output of results formatted for human consumption. The interface between the computer and the human operator is known as the user interface.

Generally, a computer consists of some form of memory for data storage, at least one element that carries out arithmetic and logic operations, and a sequencing and control element that can change the order of operations based on the information that is stored. Peripheral devices allow information to be entered from an external source, and allow the results of operations to be sent out. But modern computer had several other facilities too.

A CPU is the heart of computer that executes series of instructions that make it read, manipulate and then store data. Conditional instructions change the sequence of instructions as a function of the current state of the machine or its environment.

The first electronic **digital computers** were developed in the mid-20th century (1940–1945). Initial computers were the size of a large room, consuming as much power as several hundred modern personal computers (PCs). In this era, mechanical analog computers were used for military applications.

Modern computers based on integrated circuits are millions to billions of times more capable than the early machines, and occupy a fraction of the space. Simple computers are small enough to fit into mobile devices, and mobile computers can be powered by small batteries. Personal computers in their various forms are icons of the Information Age and are what most people think of as "computers". However, the embedded computers found in many devices from mp3 players to fighter aircraft and from toys to industrial robots are the most numerous.

Today computer replaces the Television because it facilitates all types of services which TV provides. The advent of internet has increased the scope of computer. The small application like chatting to big application like space technology are roaming with computer.

Console

The consoles are known by various names like "system console", "root console " are the text entry and display devices for system administration messages, particularly those from the BIOS or boot loader, the kernel, from the init system and from the system logger. It is a physical device consisting of a keyboard and a screen. User can directly find out the required information with the help of console with the help of some command line.

Context Free Grammar

This is the part of Automata Theory. A **context-free grammar** or **CFG** is a formal grammar in which every production rule is of the form

$$V \to w$$

- where V is a single non terminal symbol, and w is a string of terminals and/or non terminals
- w can be empty.

The languages generated by context-free grammars are known as the context-free languages.

It is important in linguistics for describing the structure of sentences and words in natural language, and in computer science for describing the structure of programming languages and other artificial languages.

Some scholars use the term **phrase structure grammar** to refer to context-free grammars, whereby phrase structure grammars are distinct from dependency grammars. Backus–Naur Form, or *BNF* is a popular notation for context-free grammars in computer science .

Context Sensitive Grammar

This is also part of Automata Theory but have opposite meaning of Context Free Grammar. A **context-sensitive grammar** or **CSG** is a formal grammar in which the left-hand sides and right-hand sides of any production rules may be surrounded by a context of terminal and nonterminal symbols. Context-sensitive grammars are more general than context-free grammars.

It was introduced by Noam Chomsky in the 1950s as a way to describe the syntax of natural language where it is indeed often the case that a word may or may not be appropriate in a certain place depending upon the context. A formal language that can be described by a context-sensitive grammar is called a context-sensitive language.

DNS

This stands for **D**omain **N**ame **S**ystem. Any server or web address is identified by the DNS. It is a hierarchical distributed naming system for computers, services, or any resource connected to the Internet or a private network. It keeps various information with domain names assigned to each of the participating entities. Most importantly, it translates domain names meaningful to humans into the numerical identifiers associated with networking equipment for the purpose of locating and addressing these devices worldwide.

An often-used analogy to explain the Domain Name System is that it serves as the phone book for the Internet by translating human-friendly computer hostnames into IP addresses. For example, the domain name *www.example.com* translates to the addresses 190.0.31.11 (IPv4) and 2621:0:201:200:10 (IPv6).

The Domain Name System makes it possible to assign domain names to groups of Internet resources and users in a meaningful way, independent of each entity's physical location. Because of this, World Wide Web (WWW) hyperlinks and Internet contact information can remain consistent and constant even if the current Internet routing arrangements change or the participant uses a mobile device.

heads over different areas of the disk when accessing a fragmented file is slower, compared to accessing the entire contents of a non-fragmented file sequentially without moving the read/write heads to seek other fragments.

Dirty Bit

This is a flag that indicates whether an attribute needs to be updated. Such situations usually occur when a bit in a memory cache or virtual memory page that has been changed by a processor but has not been updated in the storage.

CPU

This is known as heart and brain of computer. It interprets and carries out instructions provided by the software. It tests and manipulates data, and transfers information to and from other components, such as the working memory, disk drive, monitor, and keyboard. The central processing units of personal computers are generally implemented on a single chip, called a **microprocessor**.

It has several components like Motherboard, Ram, Rom, Processor etc. Several peripheral devices are connected through this like printer, scanner, sound, speaker.

Cross Compiler

The cross compiler is creates executable code for a platform other than the one on which the compiler is run. In other words, machine codes generated by one compiler are run on other machines. Cross compiler tools are used to generate executables for embedded system or multiple platforms. It is used to compile for a platform upon which it is not feasible to do the compiling, like microcontrollers that don't support an operating system. It has become more common to use this tool for para virtualization where a system may have one or more platforms in use.

Cryptography

This is the technique for secure communication in the presence of third parties. It is used while sending data from one machine to other to stop unauthorised use. More generally, it is about constructing and analyzing protocols that overcome the influence of adversaries and which are related to various aspects in information security such as confidentiality of data, and authentication. Modern cryptography intersects the disciplines of mathematics, computer science, and electrical engineering. Applications of cryptography include ATM cards, computer passwords, and commerce. There are several methods of cryptography.

Cybernetics

This is the interdisciplinary study of the structure of regulatory systems. Cybernetics is closely related to information theory, control theory and systems theory, at least in its first-order form. The second-order cybernetics has crucial methodological and epistemological implications that are fundamental to the field as a whole. Both in its origins and in its evolution in the second half of the 20th century, cybernetics is equally applicable to physical and social systems.

Cycle Redundancy Check

This is an error-detecting code commonly used in data communication in a network and storage devices to detect accidental changes to raw data. Blocks of data used in these systems get a short *check value* attached, based on the remainder of a polynomial division of their contents. On retrieval the process is repeated, and corrective action can be taken against presumed data corruption if the check values do not match.

It is called CRC because the *check* (data verification) value is a *redundancy* (it adds no information to the message) and the algorithm is based on *cyclic* codes. It is popular because they are simple to implement in binary hardware, easy to analyze mathematically, and particularly good at detecting common errors caused by noise in transmission channels. Because the check value has a fixed length, the function that generates it is occasionally used as a hash function. It was invented by W. Wesley Peterson in 1961; the 32-bit polynomial used in the CRC function of Ethernet and many other standards is the work of several researchers and was published in 1975.

Code Modulation

A code used to cause variation in a signal in accordance with a predetermined scheme, normally used to alter or modulate a carrier wave to transmit data.

Column Parity

The even or odd quality of the number of 1's or 0's in a binary code, often used to determine the integrity of data especially after transmission.

Congestion

A state occurring in part of a network when the message traffic is so heavy that it slows down network response time. This is same as the traffic congestion occurs in daily life.

Console Debugging

This is the method of finding out the bug in code through command prompt. When it is not possible to find out the bug through normal process then it is done through this.

CD-ROM

A device that writes data onto or reads data from a storage medium. It is one time writeable. The data stored in this has a long life.

CISC

This stands for complex instruction set computer. It supplies a large number of complex instructions at the assembly language level. *Assembly language* is a low-level computer **programming** language having each statement corresponds to a single machine instruction. CISC instructions facilitate the extensive manipulation of low-level computational elements and events such as memory, binary arithmetic, and addressing. This specific architectural methodology requires smaller binary files (because each CISC command accomplishes so much, relatively speaking) but involves relatively slow execution of each individual instruction (because the processor must perform more binary manipulations to each instruction). The goal of the CISC architectural philosophy is to make microprocessors easy and flexible to program and to provide for more efficient memory use.

Client/Server Architecture

This is a design of a computer **network** in which many **clients** (remote processors) request and receive service from a centralized **server** (**host computer**). This is the way on which internet or intranet is working. From any location throughout the world anybody can access any information with the help of this architecture. Client computers provide an interface to allow a computer user to request services of the server and to display the results the server returns. Servers wait for requests to arrive from clients and then respond to them.

Normally, a server provides a standardized transparent interface to clients so that clients need not be aware of the specifics of the system that is providing the service. Today clients are often situated at workstations or on personal computer, while servers are located elsewhere on the network, usually on more powerful machines. This computing model is especially effective when clients and the server each have distinct tasks that they routinely perform. In hospital data processing, for example, a client computer can be running an application program for entering patient information while the server computer is running another program that manages the database in which the information is permanently stored.

There are several layers stands between the client and server for authentic use of data as well as business purposes. Many clients can access the server's information simultaneously, and, at the same time, a client computer can perform other tasks, such as sending e-mail. Because both client and server computers are considered intelligent devices, the client-server model is completely different from the old "mainframe" model, which utilized a centralized mainframe computer that performed all the tasks for its associated "dumb" terminals.

CORBA

This stands for **C**ommon **O**bject **R**equest **B**roker **A**rchitecture. This belongs to java family.

Context Switch

This is device of switching to control the network congestion. This is the computing process of storing and restoring the state (context) of a CPU so that execution can be resumed from the same point at a later time. This enables multiple processes to share a single CPU.

This is an essential feature of a multitasking operating system. Context switches are usually computationally intensive and much of the design of operating systems is to optimize the use of context switches. A context switch can mean a register context switch, a task context switch, a thread context switch, or a process context switch. What constitutes the context is determined by the processor and the operating system. Switching from one process to another requires a certain amount of time for doing the administration—saving and loading registers and memory maps, updating various tables and list etc.

Cyber Crime

This also refers as Computer crime. It refers to any crime that involves a computer and a network. In current scenario cyber crime has emerged as a big social issue. Crimes like unauthorised access of data come under this. Some shrewd computer programmers call this — art of hacking.

A computer may be used in the commission of a crime, or it may be the target. Such crimes may threaten a nation's security and financial health. Issues surrounding this type of crimes have become high-profile, particularly those surrounding cracking, copyright infringement, child pornography, and child grooming. There are also problems of privacy when confidential information is lost or intercepted, lawfully or otherwise.

Governments throughout world setup anti cyber crime law and machinery to handle this. Internationally, both governmental and non-state actors engage in cyber-crimes, including espionage, financial theft, and other cross-border crimes. Cyber Activity crossing international borders and involving harm in the interests of at least one nation state is sometimes referred to as cyber warfare. The international legal system is attempting to hold the culprits accountable for their actions through the International Criminal Court.

Cyberspace

The core characteristic of cyberspace is that it offers an environment that consists of many participants with the ability to affect and influence each other.

This is the electronic medium of computer networks which facilitates online communication. The term was first used by the author William Gibson, though the concept was described somewhat earlier, for example in the Vernor Vinge short story "True Names." Widely used since, it has been criticized by its inventor, as Gibson himself would later describe it as an "evocative and essentially meaningless "buzzword that could serve as a cipher for all of his "cybernetic musings".

In current usage the term "cyberspace" stands for the global network of interdependent information technology infrastructures, telecommunications networks and computer processing systems. As a social experience, individuals can interact, exchange ideas, share information, provide social support, conduct business, direct actions, create artistic media, play games, engage in political discussion, and so on, using this global network. The term has become a conventional means to describe anything associated with the Internet and the diverse Internet culture. The United States government recognizes the interconnected information technology and the interdependent network of information technology infrastructures operating across this medium as part of the US National Critical Infrastructure

The first component of the term comes from "cybernetics", which is derived from the Greek word introduced by Norbert Wiener for his pioneering work in electronic communication and control science.

❑❑❑

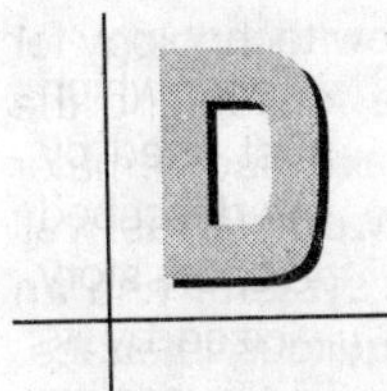

D/A Converter

This stands for Digital-to-Analog Converter. It is an equipment which converts a digital (usually binary) code to an analog signal (current, voltage, or electric charge). An analog-to-digital converter (ADC) is used for reverse operation from DAC. It is better to transmit signals into digital form due to its accuracy. DAC is needed for the signals to be recognized by human senses or other non-digital systems. It reduces the errors in data transmission as well as noise level.

Generation of audio signals from digital information in music players are common use of digital-to-analog converters. It is also used in conversion of analog signal in televisions and cell phones to display colours and shades. It enhances the picture quality.

It is exclusively manufactured on integrated circuits (ICs) due to cost and the need for matched components.

There are many DAC architectures which have different advantages and disadvantages. The suitability of a particular DAC for an application is determined by a variety of measurements including speed and resolution.

DARPA

It stands for **D**efence **A**dvanced **R**esearch **P**rojects **A**gency. It is an agency of the United States Department of Defense.

They are responsible for the development of new technology for use by the military. It has been responsible for funding the development of many technologies which have had a major effect on the world, including computer networking, as well as NLS, which was both the first hypertext system, and an important precursor to the contemporary ubiquitous interface. Originally it was named simply Advanced Research Projects Agency (ARPA), but renamed to "DARPA" specific to defence in March 1972. It was again renamed "ARPA" in February 1993, and finally renamed "DARPA" again in March 1996.

Data Abstraction

It is the process of data hiding by which data and programs are defined with a representation similar tc its pictorial meaning as rooted in the more complex realm of human life and language with their higher need of summarization and categorization, while hiding away the implementation details. It tries to reduce details so that the programmer can focus on a few concepts at a time. A system can have several abstraction layers whereby different meanings and amounts of detail are exposed to the programmer. For example, low-level abstraction layers expose details of the hardware where the program is run, while high-level layers deal with the business logic of the program. Similarly while designing database management system it helps in giving authorisation to different users based on their needs.

Database

This is an organized collection of data for one or more purposes. It keeps information which could be retrieved by the user. This is basic of internet facility. This is usually in digital form. The data are typically organized to model relevant aspects of reality (for example, the availability of rooms in guest house), in a way that supports processes requiring this information (for example, finding a guest house with vacancies). This definition is very general, and is independent of the technology used.

Today all big institutions have database because it is easier to maintain than general storage methods like book and ledger. The term "database" may be narrowed to specify particular aspects of organized collection of data and may refer to the logical database, to physical database as data content in computer data storage or to many other database sub-definitions.

The term database is correctly applied to the data and their supporting data structures, and not to the database management system. The data collection with DBMS is called a database system.

There are database administrators to handle the data. They authorise different users to access the data.

DBMS

This represents Database Management System. A database is an integrated collection of data records, files, and other objects. DBMS is a software package with computer programs that control the creation, maintenance, and use of a database. It allows institutions to conveniently develop databases for various applications with the help of database administrators (DBAs) and other specialists.

The DBMS enhances the versatility of database by allowing several user application programs to concurrently access the same database. It uses a variety of database models, such as the relational model or object model, to conveniently describe and support applications. It typically supports query languages, which are in fact high-level programming languages, dedicated database languages that considerably simplify writing database application programs.

Database languages also simplify the database organization as well as retrieving and presenting information from it. It provides facilities for controlling data access, enforcing data integrity, managing concurrency control, and recovering the database after failures and restoring it from backup files, as well as maintaining database security.

Data Bus

This is an architecture which transfers data between components inside a computer, or between computers. In early computer architecture buses were literally parallel electrical wires with multiple connections, but the term is now used for any physical arrangement that provides the same logical functionality as a parallel electrical bus. Modern Data buses can use both parallel and bit serial connections, and can be wired in either a multidrop (electrical parallel) or daisy chain topology, or connected by switched hubs, as in the case of USB.

Data Compression

This is helpful in reducing the space taken by resource in storage. The data compression, source coding or bit-rate reduction is the process of encoding information using reduced bits than the original representation would have. Compression is useful because it helps reduce the consumption of expensive resources, such as hard disk space or transmission bandwidth.

The compressed data must be decompressed to be used at other side, and this extra processing may be detrimental to some applications. The techniques used in compression of data are need based. For example, a compression scheme for video may require expensive hardware for the video to be decompressed fast enough to be viewed as it is being decompressed (the option of decompressing the video in full before watching it may be inconvenient, and requires storage space for the decompressed video).

The design of data compression schemes therefore involves various factors, including the degree of compression, the amount of distortion introduced, and the computational resources required to compress and decompress the data. There are several tools used in data compress like WinZip, War, Rar, etc.

DDL

It stands for **D**ata **D**efinition **L**anguage or **D**ata **D**escription **L**anguage. It is similar to a computer programming language for defining data structures, especially database schemas.

The concept and name was first introduced in relation to the Codasyl database model, where the schema of the database was written in a language syntax describing the records, fields, and sets of the user data model. Later it was used to refer to a subset of Structured Query Language (SQL) for creating tables and constraints. The SQL-92 introduced a schema manipulation language and schema information tables to query schemas. It is also used in a generic sense to refer to any formal language for describing data or information structures.

Data Encryption

This is the method of converting the communicating data into particular format to save it from unauthorised use. It is the converted data cannot be easily understood by unauthorized people. It is necessary to Decrypt the data on receiving end.

Decryption is the process of converting encrypted data back into its original form, so it can be understood. The use of encryption/decryption is as old as the art of communication. In war time, a cipher, often incorrectly called a code, can be employed to keep the enemy from obtaining the contents of transmissions. (Technically, a code is a means of representing a signal without the intent of keeping it secret; examples are Morse code and ASCII.) Simple ciphers include the substitution of letters for numbers, the rotation of letters in the alphabet, and the "scrambling" of voice signals by inverting the sideband frequencies.

Datagram

This is the method of sending data from one machine to other with the help of packets. Clients and servers that communicate via a perfect channel have a dedicated point-to-point channel between themselves. For communication, there must first establish the connection then transmit the data, and then close down the connection. All data sent over the channel is received in the same order that it was sent. This is guaranteed by the channel.

In contrast, clients and servers that communicate via datagram send and receive completely independent packets. These clients and servers do not have a dedicated point-to-point channel. Rather the packets are sent on their way over the network on whatever route is available.

A packet sent over a perfect channel does not contain any information about its source or its destination. The channel contains that information. In contrast, a datagram packet must contain the complete address of its source or destination (depending on if the datagram is sent or received).

Data Link Layer

The data link layer is the protocol layer that transfers data between adjacent network nodes in a wide area network or between nodes on the same local area network segment. This is Layer 2 of the seven-layer OSI model of computer networking. It corresponds to the link layer of the TCP/IP reference model.

The data link layer provides the functional and procedural means to transfer data between network entities and means to detect and possibly correct errors that may occur in the physical layer. Examples of data link protocols are Ethernet for local area networks, the Point-to-Point Protocol, HDLC and ADCCP for point-to-point connections.

The data link layer is concerned with local delivery of frames between devices on the same LAN. Data-link frames, as these protocol data units are called, do not cross the boundaries of a local network. Inter-network routing and global addressing are higher layer functions, allowing data-link protocols to focus on local delivery, addressing, and media arbitration. So, the data link layer is analogous to a neighbourhood traffic cop. It endeavours to arbitrate between parties contending for access to a medium. When devices attempt to use a medium simultaneously, frame collisions occur. Data-link protocols specify how devices detect and recover from such collisions, and may provide mechanisms to reduce or prevent them.

Data Manipulation Language

This is a syntax similar to a computer programming language and used for operations like inserting, deleting and updating data in a database. These performing read-only queries of data are sometimes also considered a component of DML. They are used for handling the database.

Structured Query Language (SQL) are popular data manipulation language, which are used to retrieve and manipulate data in a relational database. Other forms of DML are used by IMS/DLI, CODASYL databases, such as IDMS and others.

Data manipulation language comprises the SQL data change statements, which modify stored data but not the schema or database objects. Manipulation of persistent database objects, e.g., tables or stored procedures, via the SQL schema statements, rather than the data stored within them, is considered to be part of a separate data definition language. In SQL, these two categories are similar in their detailed syntax, data types, expressions etc., but distinct in their over all function.

Data Matrix

This is a two-dimensional matrix consisting of black and white "cells" or modules arranged in rectangular pattern. Depending on the situation a "light" module is a 0 and a "dark" module is a 1, or vice versa. The information to be encoded can be text or raw data.

The data size in data matrix is from a few bytes up to 1556 bytes. The length of the encoded data depends on the dimension used. A Data Matrix symbol can store up to 2,335 alpha-numeric characters.

Every Data Matrix is composed of two solid adjacent borders in an "L" shape called the "finder pattern" and two other borders consisting of alternating dark and light "cells" or modules called the "timing pattern". Within these borders are the rows and columns of cells encoding information. The finder pattern is used to locate and orient the symbol while the timing pattern provides a count of the number of rows and columns in the symbol.

Data Processing

It is generally known as Computer data processing. It is most important part in data communication. This is the process that a computer program does to enter data and summarise, analyse or otherwise convert data into usable information. The process may be automated and run on a computer or any other such machines. It involves recording, analysing, sorting, summarising, calculating, disseminating and storing data.

Since data are most useful when well-presented and actually *informative*, data-processing systems are often referred to as information systems. The terms are roughly synonymous, performing similar conversions; data-processing systems typically manipulate raw data into information, and likewise information systems typically take raw data as input to produce information as output.

It may or may not be differentiated from data conversion, when the process is merely to convert data to another format, and does not involve any data manipulation.

Data Multiplexer

This is also known as "mux" and Data Selector. It is a device that selects one of several analog or digital input signals and forwards the selected input into a single line output. A multiplexer of 2^n inputs has n select lines, which are used to select which input line to send to the output.

This is mainly used to increase the amount of data that can be sent over the network within a certain amount of time and bandwidth.

It is easy to send one signal than several. An electronic multiplexer makes it possible for several signals to share one device or resource, for example one A/D converter or one communication line, instead of having one device per input signal.

Data Structure

This is a method of storing and organizing data in a computer so that it can be used efficiently and easily. There are different kinds of data structures present to different kinds of applications. Some are highly specialized to specific tasks. For example, B-trees are particularly well-suited for implementation of databases, while compiler implementations usually use hash tables to look up identifiers. There are several algorithms to support data structure access like Stack, List, Tree etc.

This is used in almost every program or software system. Data structures provide means to manage huge amounts of data efficiently, such as large databases and internet indexing services. Usually, efficient data structures are key to designing efficient algorithms. Some formal design methods and programming languages emphasize data structures, rather than algorithms, as the key organizing factor in software design.

Deadlock

This is an incident where two or more competing actions are each waiting for the other to finish, and thus neither ever does. It is seen like the "chicken or the egg" phrase. This is like waiting of two trains to move on same line in opposite directions. There are four conditions for deadlock in computer science like Mutual Exclusion, Cyclic waiting etc.

The **Coffman deadlock** refers to a specific condition when two or more processes are each waiting for the other to release a resource, or more than two processes are waiting for resources in a circular chain.

This is a common problem in multiprocessing. There are several algorithms for avoiding deadlock condition. Computers intended for the *time-sharing* and/or *real-time* markets are often equipped with a *hardware lock*, which guarantees *exclusive access* to processes, forcing serialized access. Deadlocks are particularly troubling because there is no *general* solution to avoid deadlocks.

This situation may be like that of two people who are drawing diagrams, with only one pencil and one ruler between them. If one person takes the pencil and the other takes the ruler, a deadlock occurs when the person with the pencil needs the ruler and the person with the ruler needs the pencil to finish his work with the ruler. Neither request can be satisfied, so a deadlock occurs.

The Coffman deadlock description of deadlock are stronger than telecommunications because processes can wait for messages instead of resources. A deadlock can be the result of corrupt messages or signals rather than merely waiting for resources. For example, a dataflow element that has been directed to receive input on the wrong link will never proceed even though that link is not involved in a Coffman cycle.

Debugging

This is a methodical process of digging out and reducing the number of bugs, or defects, in a computer program or a piece of electronic hardware so that it behave as expected.

It tends to be harder when various subsystems are tightly coupled, as changes in one may cause bugs to emerge in another. There are several ways of debugging like manual debugging, console debugging etc. Even today there are several tools available in market to find out the bug. It is necessary to find out the bug because without doing this, no software will run.

Decision Table

This is used for reaching on conclusion like flowcharts, if-then-else, switch-case statements, associate conditions with actions to perform etc.

In the 1960s and 1970s a range of "decision table based" languages such as File tab were popular for business programming.

Each decision corr-esponds to a variable, relation or predicate whose possible values are listed among the condition alternatives. Each action is a procedure or operation to perform,

THE FOUR QUADRANTS	
Conditions	Condition alternatives
Actions	Action entries

and the entries specify whether (or in what order) the action is to be performed for the set of condition alternatives the entry corresponds to.

Many decision tables include in their condition alternatives the don't care symbol, a hyphen. Using don't cares can simplify decision tables, especially when a given condition has little influence on the actions to be performed. In some cases, entire conditions thought to be important initially are found to be irrelevant when none of the conditions influence which actions are performed.

Aside from the basic four quadrant structure, decision tables vary widely in the way the condition alternatives and action entries are represented. Some decision tables use simple true/false values to represent the alternatives to a condition, other tables may use numbered alternatives, and some tables even use fuzzy logic or probabilistic representations for condition alternatives. In a similar way, action entries can simply represent whether an action is to be performed, or in more advanced decision tables, the sequencing of actions to perform.

Demand Paging

This is opposed to Anticipatory Paging. This is an application part of virtual memory. The system which uses demand paging, the operating system copies a disk page into physical memory. If particular page did not found in memory then it is known as Page Fault.

It follows that a process begins execution with none of its pages in physical memory, and many page faults will occur until most of a process's working set of pages is located in physical memory. This is an example of lazy loading techniques.

It follows that pages which should only be brought into memory if the executing process demands them. This is often referred to as lazy evaluation as only those pages demanded by the process are swapped from secondary storage to main memory. When a process is to be swapped into main memory for processing, the pager guesses which pages will be used prior to the process being swapped out again. The pager will only load these pages into memory. This process avoids loading pages that are unlikely to be used and focuses on pages needed during the current process execution period. Therefore, not only is unnecessary page load during swapping avoided but we also try to pre-empt which pages will be needed and avoid loading pages during execution.

de Morgan's Law

This is rule relating the logical operators "and" and "or" in terms of each other via negation. With two operands A and B. This is notified as

$$\overline{A \cdot B} = \overline{A} + \overline{B}$$

$$\overline{A + B} = \overline{A} \cdot \overline{B}$$

We can also write it as

NOT (A OR B) = (NOT A) AND (NOT B)

NOT (A AND B) = (NOT A) OR (NOT B)

Demultiplexer

It decodes the signal sent by Multiplexer by taking one data input from a number of selection inputs, and convert them into multiple one as it was as at the time of input to multiplexer. They forward the data input to one of the outputs depending on the values of the selection inputs. Demultiplexers are sometimes convenient for designing general purpose logic, because if the Demultiplexer's input is always true. It acts as a decoder. The Multiplexer and Demultiplexer are always used in pair.

The Diagram of Demultiplexer:

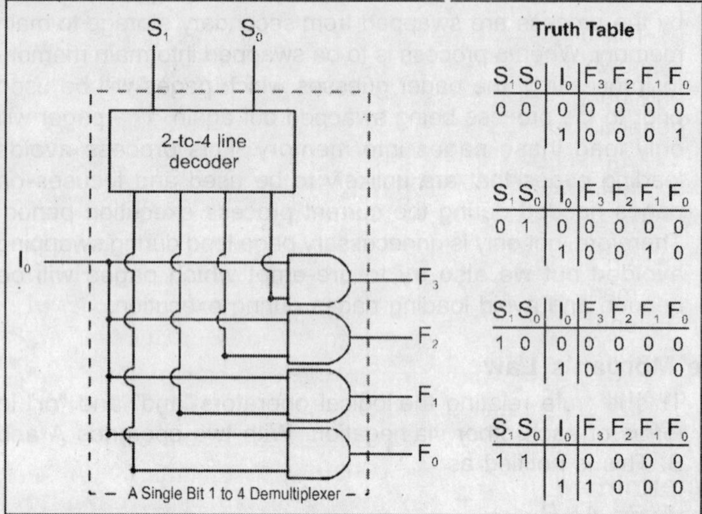

Truth Table

S_1 S_0	I_0	F_3 F_2 F_1 F_0
0 0	0	0 0 0 0
	1	0 0 0 1

S_1 S_0	I_0	F_3 F_2 F_1 F_0
0 1	0	0 0 0 0
	1	0 0 1 0

S_1 S_0	I_0	F_3 F_2 F_1 F_0
1 0	0	0 0 0 0
	1	0 1 0 0

S_1 S_0	I_0	F_3 F_2 F_1 F_0
1 1	0	0 0 0 0
	1	1 0 0 0

Depth First Search

This is an algorithm of searching data in database. This is an uninformed search that progresses by expanding the first child node of the search tree that appears and thus going deeper and deeper until a goal node is found, or until it hits a node that has no children. Then the search backtracks, returning to the most recent node it hasn't finished exploring. In a non-recursive implementation, all freshly expanded nodes are added to a stack for exploration

Deque

This is known as Double-Ended Queue. This is an abstract data type which implements a queue for which elements can be added or removed from the front (head) or back (tail). It is also called a Head-Tail linked list.

This differs from the normal queue abstract data type which is known as First-In-First-Out List (FIFO), where elements can only be added to one end and removed from the other. This general data class has some possible sub-types:

- An input-restricted deque is one where deletion can be made from both ends, but insertion can only be made at one end.
- An output-restricted deque is one where insertion can be made at both ends, but deletion can be made from one end only.

Both the basic and most common list types in computing, queues and stacks can be considered specializations of deques, and can be implemented using deques.

Deterministic Language

This is a formal language which is defined by a deterministic context-free grammar. The set of deterministic context-free languages is known as DCFL. This is identical to the set of languages accepted by a deterministic pushdown automaton.

The set of deterministic languages is a proper subset of the set of that possess an unambiguous context free grammar. For example, the language of even-length palindromes on the alphabet of 0 and 1 has the simple, unambiguous grammar S > 0S0 I 1S1 I å, but it cannot be parsed by a deterministic push down automaton.

The languages of this class have practical importance in computer science while creating Compiler and Interpreter. The complexity of the program and execution of a deterministic pushdown automaton is vastly less than that of a non-deterministic one. In the naive implementation, it must make copies of the stack every time a non-deterministic step occurs.

The best known algorithm to test membership in any context-free language is Valiant's algorithm, taking $O(n^{2.378})$

time, whereas membership in a deterministic context-free language can be tested in O(*n*) time, where n is the length of the string.

The deterministic context-free languages are exactly those recognized by some LR grammar

Digital Computer

This is a computer that stores data in terms of binary numbers and proceeds in discrete steps from one state to the next. In digital computers, even letters, words and whole texts are represented digitally. Unlike analog computer, digital computers can only approximate a continuum by assigning large numbers of digits to a state description and by proceeding in arbitrarily small steps. The performance of digital computer are better than analog computer.

Diode

This is a type of two-terminal electronic device with *non-linear* conductance. This characteristic distinguishing it from components such as two-terminal linear resistors which obey Ohm's law. The most common function of a diode is to allow an electric current to pass in one direction (called the diode's *forward* direction), while blocking current in the opposite direction (the *reverse* direction). Thus, the diode can be thought of as an electronic version of a check valve. This unidirectional behaviour is called rectification, and is used to convert alternating current to direct current, and to extract modulation from radio signals in radio receivers — these diodes are forms of rectifiers.

There are several types of diodes. A semiconductor diode, the most common type today, is a crystalline piece of semiconductor material connected to two electrical terminals. A vacuum tube diode is a vacuum tube with two electrodes: a plate and a cathode.

Disjunction

This is also known as Inclusive Disjunction or Alternation. Its results are true whenever *one or more* of its operands are true. E.g. in this context, "*C* or D" is true if *C* is true, or if D is true, or if both C and D are true. In grammar, **or** is a coordinating conjunction.

In ordinary language, i.e. outside of contexts such as formal logic, mathematics and programming, "or" sometimes has the meaning of exclusive disjunction. E.g. "Please call me or send an email" means "do one or the other, but not both". On the other hand, "Her marks are so good that she's either very bright or studies hard" allows for the possibility that the person is both bright and works hard. In other words, in ordinary language 'or' can mean inclusive or exclusive or. Usually it is clear from the context which is the intended meaning.

Distributed Database

This is a database in which storage devices are not all placed to a common CPU. It may be stored in several stations located in the same physical location, or may be dispersed over a network of interconnected computers.

A database can be distributed across multiple physical locations. It can reside on a network server on the Internet or on corporate intranets/extranets, or on other company networks. The replication and distribution of databases improves database performance at end-user worksites.

There are two processes — replication and duplication to assure the effectiveness of database. Replication involves using specialized software that looks for changes in the distributive database. Once the changes have been identified, the replication process makes all the databases look the same. The replication process can be very complex and time-consuming depending on the size and number of the distributive databases. This process may also require a lot of time and computer resources. Duplication on the other hand is not as complicated. It basically identifies one database as a master and then duplicates of that database. The duplication process is normally done at a set time after hours. This is to ensure that each distributed location has the same data. In the duplication process, changes to the master database only are allowed. This is to ensure that local data will not be overwritten. Both of the processes can keep the data current in all distributive locations.

Divide and Conquer Algorithm

This is an algorithm for searching the data in database. It is based on multi-branched recursion. It works by recursively breaking down a problem into two or more sub-problems of the same (or related) type, until these become simple enough to be solved directly. The solutions to the sub-problems are then combined to give a solution to the original problem.

This technique is used for efficient algorithms of all kinds of problems, such as — sorting (e.g., quick sort, merge sort), multiplying large numbers (e.g. Karatsuba), syntactic analysis (e.g., top-down parsers), and computing the discrete Fourier transform (FFTs).

The name "divide and conquer" is sometimes also applied to algorithms that reduce each problem to only one sub problem, such as the binary search algorithm for finding a record in a sorted list. These algorithms can be implemented more efficiently than general divide-and-conquer algorithms; in particular, if they use tail recursion, they can be converted into simple loops.. Under this broad definition, however, every algorithm that uses recursion or loops could be regarded as a "divide and conquer algorithm". Therefore, some authors consider that the name "divide and conquer" should be used only when each problem may generate two or more sub- problems. The name decrease and conquer has been proposed instead for the single sub-problem class.

Dope Vector

This is a data structure used to hold information about a data object, e.g., an array, especially its memory layout. It contains information about the type of array element, rank of an array, the extents of an array, and the stride of an array as well as a pointer to the block in memory containing the array elements. It is also used in compilers to pass entire arrays between procedures in a high level language like Fortran. Till the invention of the linked-list, a dope vector was used internally in the internal structure of computer systems. The dope vector included a identifier, a length, a parent address, and a next child address. The identifier was an assigned name and was mostly useless, but the length was the amount of allocated storage to this vector from the end of the dope vector that contained data of use to the internal processes of the computer. This length was called the offset, span of vector length. The parent and child references were absolute core references, or register and offset settings to the parent or child depending on the type of computer. Dope vectors were managed internally by the operating system and allowed the processor to allocate and de-allocate storage in specific segments as needed.

DOS

This is an operating system. It is the most commonly used member of the DOS family of operating systems. It works on command prompt and do not have attractive look like other operating systems. But it is still used for large data manipulation. This was the main operating system for IBM PC compatible personal computers during the 1980s to the mid 1990s, till it was gradually superseded by operating systems offering a graphical user interface (GUI), in particular by various generations of the Microsoft Windows operating system.

Microsoft quickly bought the rights to QDOS (Quick and Disc Operating System), also known as 86-DOS, from Seattle Computer Products, and began work on modifying it to meet IBM's specification. The first edition, MS-DOS 1.0, was launched in 1982. The version shipped with IBM's PCs was called PC DOS. Although MS-DOS and PC-DOS were initially developed in parallel by Microsoft and IBM, the two products eventually went their separate ways.

Ultimately it was the key product in Microsoft's growth from a programming languages company to a diverse software development firm, providing the company with essential revenue and marketing resources. It was also the underlying basic operating system on which early versions of Windows ran as a GUI.

Double Link List

This is a linked data structure that consists of a set of sequentially linked records called nodes. Each node contains two fields, called *links*, that are references to the previous and to the next node in the sequence of nodes. The beginning and ending nodes' **previous** and **next** links, respectively, point to some kind of terminator, typically a sentinel node or null, to facilitate traversal of the list. If there is only one sentinel node, then the list is circularly linked via the sentinel node. It can be conceptualized as two singly linked lists formed from the same data items, but in opposite sequential orders. Pictorially it can be seen as:

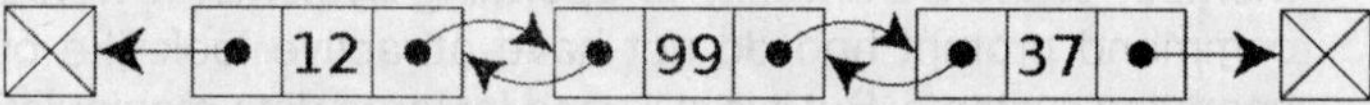

The two node links allow traversal of the list in either direction. While adding or removing a node in a doubly linked list requires changing more links than the same operations on a singly linked list, the operations are simpler and potentially more efficient (for nodes other than first nodes) because there is no need to keep track of the previous node during traversal or no need to traverse the list to find the previous node, so that its link can be modified.

DTL

This stands for Diode–transistor logic. It is framed through diode and transistor. It is a class of digital circuits that is the direct ancestor of transistor–transistor logic. It is called so because the logic gating function (e.g., AND) is performed by a diode network and the amplifying function is performed by a transistor (contrast this with RTL and TTL).

D-Flip-flop

This is the most common flip-flop in use. It is also known as *data* or *delay* flip-flop because its output Q looks like a delay of input D. The Q output takes on the state of the D input at the moment of a positive edge at the clock pin (or negative edge if the clock input is active low).

TRUTH TABLE OF D-FLIP-FLOP

Clock	*D*	*Q*	*Q_{prev}*
Rising	0	0	X
Rising edge	1	1	X
Non-Rising	X	Q_{prev}	

It is called the D flip-flop for this reason, since the output takes the value of the D input or *data* input, and *delays* it by one clock cycle. The D flip-flop can be interpreted as a primitive memory cell, zero-order hold, or delay line. Whenever the clock pulses, the value of Q_{next} is D and Q_{prev} otherwise.

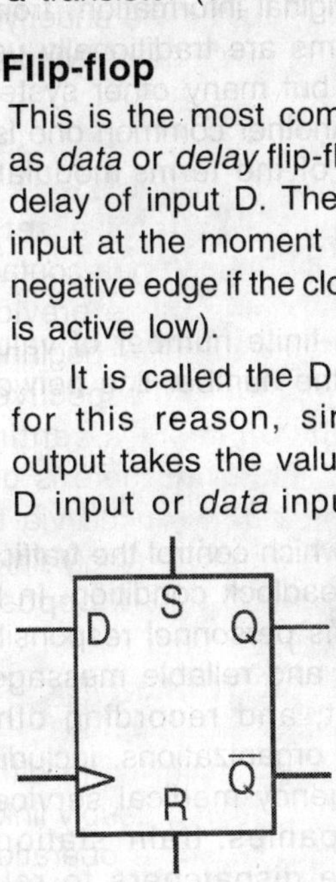

D S Q
$\overline{Q}$ R

Where 'X' denotes a *Don't care* condition.

Data Format

This refers to the way the data is put together. Pictures, or more technically advanced images, are stored in various formats such as bmp, jpg, gif and png.These letters are placed after a dot and are called the filename extension. So in the case of *example.bmp* this refers to a file called *example* stored in *bmp* (bitmap) format, *gif* is a slim line format taking less storage space and hence holding less detail than *bmp*.

Demodulation

This is an electronic circuit or computer program that is used to recover the information content from the modulated wave. This is the way of extracting the original information from a modulated carrier wave. These terms are traditionally used in connection with radio receivers, but many other systems use many kinds of demodulators. Another common one is in a modem, which is a contraction of the terms modulator/ demodulator.

Discrete Data

A type of data, if there are only a finite number of values possible or if there is a space on the number line between each 2 possible values.

Dispatcher

This is a programme or instrument which control the traffic of network. It even try to avoid the deadlock condition. In lay man term, these are communications personnel responsible for receiving and transmitting pure and reliable messages, tracking vehicles and equipment, and recording other important information. A number of organizations, including police and fire departments, emergency medical services, taxicab providers, trucking companies, train stations, and public utility companies, use dispatchers to relay information and coordinate their operations. Essentially, the dispatcher is the "conductor" of the force, and is responsible for the direction of all units within it.

Data Authentication

This is the technique of verifying data as well as giving permission to use the data.

Data Flow Diagram

This is a graphical representation of the "flow" of data through an information system. They have step by step information about any action to achieve certain goal. Often they are a preliminary step used to create an overview of the system which can later be elaborated. DFDs can also be used for the visualization of data processing (structured design).

A DFD shows what kinds of data will be input to and output from the system, where the data will come from and go to, and where the data will be stored. It does not show information about the timing of processes, or information about whether processes will operate in sequence or in parallel (which is shown on a flowchart).

Defragmentation

This is a process that reduces the amount of fragmentation. It helps in freeing the unused memory at one place rather than scattered. It does this by physically organizing the contents of the mass storage device used to store files into the smallest number of contiguous regions. It also attempts to create larger regions of free space using *compaction* to impede the return of fragmentation. Some defragmentation utilities try to keep smaller files within a single directory together, as they are often accessed in sequence.

Defragmentation is advantageous and relevant to file systems on electromechanical disk drives. The movement of the hard drive's read/write heads over different areas of the disk when accessing fragmented files is slower, compared to accessing the entire contents of a non-fragmented file sequentially without moving the read/write heads to seek other fragments.

Dirty Bit

This is a flag that indicates whether an attribute needs to be updated. Such situations usually occur when a bit in a memory cache or virtual memory page that has been changed by a processor but has not been updated in the storage.

DNS

This stands for **D**omain **N**ame **S**ystem. Any server or web address is identified by the DNS. It is a hierarchical distributed naming system for computers, services, or any resource connected to the Internet or a private network. It keeps various information with domain names assigned to each of the participating entities. Most importantly, it translates domain names meaningful to humans into the numerical identifiers associated with networking equipment for the purpose of locating and addressing these devices worldwide.

An often-used analogy to explain the Domain Name System is that it serves as the phone book for the Internet by translating human-friendly computer hostnames into IP addresses. For example, the domain name *www.example.com* translates to the addresses 190.0.31.11 (IPv4) and 2621:0: 201:200:10 (IPv6).

The Domain Name System makes it possible to assign domain names to groups of Internet resources and users in a meaningful way, independent of each entity's physical location. Because of this, World Wide Web (WWW) hyperlinks and Internet contact information can remain consistent and constant even if the current Internet routing arrangements change or the participant uses a mobile device.

DRAM

It stands for Dynamic random-access memory. It is a type of random-access memory that stores each bit of data in a separate capacitor within an integrated circuit. The capacitor can be either charged or discharged; these two states are taken to represent the two values of a bit, conventionally called 0 and 1. Since capacitors leak charge, the information eventually fades unless the capacitor charge is refreshed periodically. Because of this refresh requirement, it is a *dynamic* memory as opposed to SRAM and other *static* memory.

❑ ❑ ❑

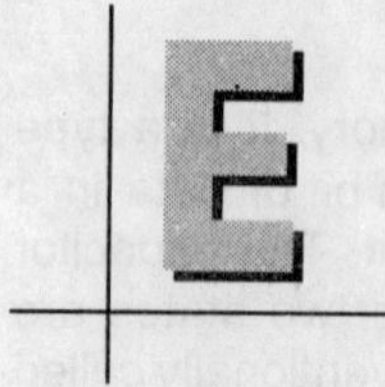

EBCDIC

This stands for **E**xtended **B**inary **C**oded **D**ecimal **I**nterchange **C**ode. It is an 8-bit character encoding used mainly on mainframe and midrange computer operating systems. It was framed in 1963 and 1964 by IBM with announcememt of the release with of the IBM System/360 line of mainframe computers. It was developed separately from, the 7-bit ASCII encoding scheme.

It descended from the code used with punched cards and the corresponding six bit binary-coded decimal code used with most of computer peripherals of the late 1950s and early 1960s. It is an 8-bit character encoding, in contrast to, and It extend the existing binary-coded decimal (BCD) interchange code, or BCDIC, which itself was devised as an efficient means of encoding the two *zone* and *number* punches on punched cards into 6 bits.

EEPROM

It stands for **E**lectrically **E**rasable **P**rogrammable **ROM**. This is rewritable memory chip that holds its content without power. These are bit or byte addressable at the write level. It means either the bit or byte must be erased before it can be re-written.

The flash memory is almost identical in architecture of this, an entire block of bytes must be erased before writing. In addition, EEPROMs are typically used on circuit boards to store small amounts of instructions and data, whereas flash memory modules hold gigabytes of data for digital camera storage and hard disk replacements.

Eigen Vector

The prefix **Eigen-** is adopted from the German word "Eigen" for "own" in the sense of a characteristic description. It is also known as **characteristic vectors**. The **Eigen vectors** represents non-zero vectors of a square matrix, after being multiplied by the matrix and remain parallel to the original vector. For each eigenvector, the corresponding Eigen value is the factor by which the eigenvector is scaled when multiplied by the matrix. Similarly, the Eigen values are also known as characteristic values.

The numerical expression of this is as follows:

If A is a square matrix, a non-zero vector V is an eigen vector of A if there is a scalar λ (lambda) such that $AV = \lambda V$

The scalar λ (lambda) is said to be the Eigen value of A corresponding to V.

However, the zero vector is not an eigen vector. These ideas often are extended to more general situations, where scalars are elements of any field, vectors are elements of any vector space, and linear transformations may or may not be represented by matrix multiplication. For example, instead of real numbers, scalars may be complex numbers; instead of arrows, vectors may be functions or frequencies; instead of matrix multiplication, linear transformations may be operators such as the derivatives from calculus. These are only a few of countless examples where eigen vectors and Eigen values are important.

In such cases, the concept of *direction* loses its ordinary meaning, and is given an abstract definition. Even so, if that abstract *direction* is unchanged by a given linear transformation, the prefix "eigen" is used, as in *Eigen function*, *Eigen mode*, Eigen, *eigen state*, and *Eigen frequency*.

Electronic Mail

A system for sending and receiving messages electronically over a data network with the help of communicating device like mobile, computer etc. This is prevalent way of keeping in touch with others in modern environment.

Encapsulation

In a programming world **encapsulation** is used to refer to one of two related but distinct functions. It is:

- A language mechanism for restricting access to some of the object's components.
- A language construct that facilitates the bundling of data with the methods (or other functions) operating on that data.

Some practitioner and academics use the first meaning alone or in combination with the second as a distinguishing feature of object oriented programming, while other which provide lexical closures view encapsulation as a feature of the language orthogonal to object orientation. The second definition is motivated by the fact that in many OOP languages hiding of components is not automatic or can be overridden; thus, information hiding is defined as a separate notion by those who prefer the second definition, e.g.,

```
Multiplication(int a, char b)
{ }
Multiplication(int  a, char b, int c)
{ }
```

Both have same function name but they may have different meaning.

Encoding

This is the method of converting data from one format to another. There are several such techniques present like BCD, EBCD etc.

Encryption

This is the method of converting the communicating data into particular format to save it from unauthorised use. It is the converted data that cannot be easily understood by unauthorized people. It is necessary to Decrypt the data on receiving end.

Decryption is the process of converting encrypted data back into its original form, so it can be understood. The use of encryption/decryption is as old as the art of communication. In wartime, a cipher, often incorrectly called a code, can be employed to keep the enemy from obtaining the contents of transmissions. (Technically, a code is a means of representing a signal without the intent of keeping it secret; examples are Morse code and ASCII.) Simple ciphers include the substitution of letters for numbers, the rotation of letters in the alphabet, and the "scrambling" of voice signals by inverting the sideband frequencies.

End-around-carry

This is a carry from the most significant digit place to the least significant digit place.

Entropy

There are two types of Entropy- Positive and negative. This is the randomness collected by an operating system or application for use in cryptography or other uses that require random data. This randomness is often collected from hardware sources, either pre-existing ones such as mouse movements or specially provided randomness generators.

Enumeration

This is used in programming language such as java and C++.

It also used in mathematics and theoretical computer science. The broadest and most abstract definition of an enumeration of a set is an exact listing of all of its elements (perhaps with repetition). The restrictions imposed on the type of list used depend on the branch of mathematics and the context in which one is working. In more specific settings, this notion of enumeration encompasses the two different types of listing—one where there is a natural ordering and one where the ordering is more nebulous. These two different kinds of enumerations correspond to a procedure for listing all members of the set in some definite sequence, or a count of objects of a specified kind, respectively. While the two kinds of enumeration often overlap in most natural situations, they can assume very different meanings in certain contexts.

EPROM

It stands for Erasable Programmable Memory. This is a type of memory chip that retains its data when its power supply is switched off. We can say, it is non-volatile. It consist of an array of floating-gate transistors individually programmed by an electronic device that supplies higher voltages than those normally used in digital circuits.

Once programmed, an EPROM can be erased by exposing it to strong ultraviolet light from a mercury-vapour light source. It is opposite of EEROM.

Ethernet

This belongs to family of computer networking technologies for local area networks (LANs), which commercially introduced in 1980. Ethernet has largely replaced competing wired LAN technologies. Systems communicating over Ethernet divide a stream of data into individual packets called frames. Where each frame contains source and destination addresses and error-checking data so that damaged data can be detected and re-transmitted.

The standards of it define several wiring and signalling variants. The original 10BASE5 Ethernet used coaxial cable as a shared medium while the coaxial cables were replaced by twisted pair and fiber optic links in conjunction with hubs or switches. Data rates were periodically increased from the original 10 megabits per second, to 100 gigabits per second. Since its commercial release, Ethernet has retained a good degree of compatibility. Features such as the 48-bit MAC address and Ethernet frame format have influenced other networking protocols.

Euclid's Algorithm

This is also known as Euclidean algorithm. This is an efficient method for computing the greatest common divisor (GCD) of two integers, also known as the greatest common factor (GCF) or highest common factor (HCF). This is named after its inventor Euclid.

The GCD of two numbers is the largest number that divides both of them without leaving a remainder. The Euclidean algorithm is based on the principle that the greatest common divisor of two numbers does not change if the smaller number is subtracted from the larger number.

The original algorithm was described only for natural numbers and geometric lengths (real numbers), but the algorithm was generalized in the 19th century to other types of numbers, such as Gaussian integers and polynomials in one variable. This led to modern abstract algebraic notions such as Euclidean domains. The Euclidean algorithm has been generalized further to other mathematical structures, such as knots and multivariate polynomials.

Exclusive-NOR gate

This is opposite to the X-OR gate. It will give a low output if either, but not both,

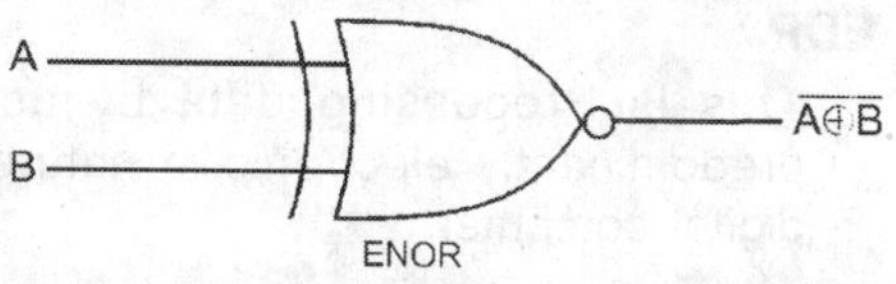

A

B

$\overline{A \oplus B}$

ENOR

of its two inputs are high. The symbol is an X-OR gate with a small circle on the output. The small circle represents inversion. It could be framed by universal gate.

2 Input EXNOR gate

A	B	$\overline{A \oplus B}$
0	0	1
0	1	0
1	0	0
1	1	1

Exclusive-OR gate

The Exclusive-OR-gate is similar to an OR-gate. It can have an arbitrary number of inputs, and its output value is 1 if and only if exactly one input is 1 (and thus the others 0). Otherwise, the output is 0.

We can draw an exclusive-or-gate like this:

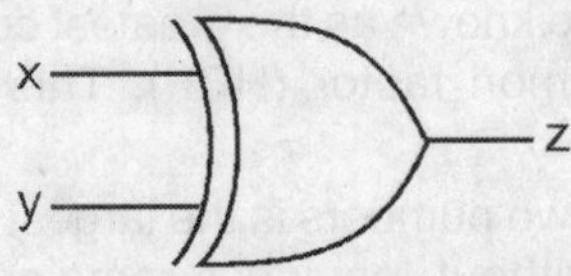

The truth table for an exclusive-or-gate with two inputs looks like this:

x	y	|	z
-	-	-	-
0	0	|	0
0	1	|	1
1	0	|	1
1	1	|	

EBCD Code

It stands for **E**xtended **B**inary **C**oded **D**ecimal. It is also a coding techniques.

EDP

This is Processing data by using equipment that is predominantly electronic in nature, such as an electronic digital computer.

EFTS

This stands for **E**lectronic **F**und **T**ransfer **S**ystem. This is technology online transaction with the help of internet. It reduces the human effort in data transaction. Almost all financial institution are today giving this facility to their customer.

Electron Gun

The part of a cathode-ray tube that emits a narrow beam of electrons, consisting of a cathode, control grids, and usually a heater. Electrons are emitted from the cathode, which is typically heated by electric current to give the electrons escape energy. The electrons are then focused into a beam by the electric fields of the control grids.

ECL

This stands for **E**mitter **C**oupled **C**ircuit.

Error Recovery Procedure

Error detection is commonly realized through a suitable hash function or checksum algorithm. A hash function adds a fixed-length *tag* to the message, which enables receivers to verify the delivered message by recompiling the tag and comparing it with the one provided.

There exists a variety of different hash function methods. Some are of particularly widespread use because of either their simplicity or their suitability for detecting certain kinds of errors (e.g., the cyclic redundancy check's performance in detecting burst errors).

Random-error-correcting codes based on minimum distance coding can provide a suitable alternative to hash functions when a strict guarantee on the minimum number of errors to be detected is desired. Repetition codes, described below, are special cases of error-correcting codes: although rather inefficient, they find applications for both error correction and detection due to their simplicity.

Even Parity Check

This is the parity-checking mode in which each set of transmitted bits must have an even number of set bits. The parity checking system on the sending side ensures even parity by setting the extra *parity bit* if necessary.

Exponential Function

This is a function in which a constant base is raised to a variable power. Exponential functions are used to model changes in population size, in the spread of diseases, and in the growth of investments. It can also accurately predict types of decline typified by radioactive decay. The essence of exponential growth, and a characteristic of all exponential growth functions, is that they double in size over regular intervals. The most important exponential function is e^x, the inverse of the natural logarithmic function. The base of exponential function in *'e'*.

EARN

This stands for European Academic Research Network.

e-Business/e-Commerce

This is a term used to describe businesses or commerce roaming on the Internet or intranet. It utilizes Internet technologies to improve the productivity or profitability of a business. In a lay men term, it may be used to describe any form of electronic business —- that is to say, any business which utilizes a computer or any other such communicating device like gazette.

It is preferred in selling products online. The most common implementation of e-business is as an additional, or in some cases primary, storefront. By selling products and services online, an e-business is able to reach a much wider consumer base than any traditional brick-and-mortar store could ever hope for. This function of e-business is referred to as e-commerce, and the terms are occasionally used interchangeably.

An e-business may also use the Internet to acquire wholesale products or supplies for in-house production. This facet of e-business is sometimes referred to as e-procurement, and may offer businesses the opportunity to cut their costs dramatically. Even many e-businesses which operate without an electronic storefront now use e-procurement as a way to better track and manage their purchasing.

Echoplex

This is a tape delay effect, designed by Mike Battle in 1959. Echoplex set a standard for the effect in the 1960s and was used by some of the most notable guitar players of the era.

Exe

This stands for Executable file. This is the extension of file system. It indicates that when this file will run, it will install the respective application on computer. It comes with several other files.

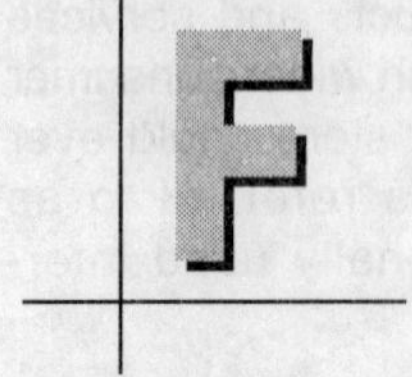

Facsimile

This is a copy or reproduction of an old document like map, art, manuscript print, or other item of historical value that is as true to the original source as possible.

It attempting to replicate the source as accurately as possible in terms of scale, colour, condition, and other material qualities, that's why it had different significance from other copying techniques. The incomplete copy is a "partial facsimile". This is used, by scholars to research a source that they do not have access to otherwise and by museums and archives for museum and media preservation. Many are sold commercially, often accompanied by a volume of commentary.

Fan-in

The maximum number of inputs lines to a logic or logic device is known as Fan-in.

Fan-out

The maximum number of devices that can be safely driven by the output from a logic gate or logic device.

FDM

This stands for Frequency-division multiplexing. It is a method of signal multiplexing which involves assigning non-overlapping frequency ranges to different signals or to each "user" of a medium. The multiplexing is done on frequency. It combines all the incoming frequencies in a single line and transmit to other side, where it again demultiplex to retrieve the actual one.

FDMA

This stands for Frequency Division Multiple Access. This is a protocol. This is a channel access method used in multiple-access protocols as a channelization protocol. It gives users an individual allocation of one or several frequency bands, or channels. It is common in satellite communication. FDMA, like other Multiple Access systems, coordinates access between multiple users. The alternatives of this are TDMA, CDMA, or SDMA. These protocols are utilized differently, at different levels of the theoretical OSI model.

But there are a disadvantage with this – Crosstalk may cause interference among frequencies and disrupt the transmission.

Flip-Flop

This is also known as **latch.** This is a circuit that has two stable states and can be used to store state information. This is used as storing the data..

The circuit can be made to change state by signals applied to one or more control inputs and will have one or two outputs. It is the basic storage element in sequential logic. It is a fundamental building block of digital electronic systems used in computers, communications, and many other types of systems.

When used in a finite-state machine, the output and next state depend not only on its current input, but also on its current state (and hence, previous inputs). It can also be used for counting of pulses, and for synchronizing variably-timed input signals to some reference timing signal.

There are two types of Flip-flops either simple (transparent or opaque) or clocked (synchronous or edge-triggered).The simple ones are commonly called latches. The word *latch* is mainly used for storage elements, while clocked devices are described as *flip-flops.*

The other types are J-K Flip-flop, T-Flip- Flop etc.

Fiber Optics

This is an instrument of transmitting information from one place to another by sending pulses of light through a fiber. It functions on total reflection of light. The light forms an electromagnetic carrier wave that is modulated to carry information. The speed of signal in fiber optics transmits much faster than other medium.

It was first developed in the 1970s. The fiber-optic communication systems have revolutionized the telecommunications industry and have played a major role in the advent of the Information Age. Because of its advantages over electrical transmission, optical fibers have largely replaced copper wire communications in core networks in the developed world.

The process of communicating using fiber-optics involves the following basic steps: Creating the optical signal involving the use of a transmitter, relaying the signal along the fiber, ensuring that the signal does not become too distorted or weak, receiving the optical signal, and converting it into an electrical signal.

Fibonacci Series

These are the numbers in the following integer sequence:
0, 1, 1, 2, 3, 5, 8, 13, 21, 34, 55. 89, 144, ...

By definition, the first two numbers in the Fibonacci sequence are 0 and 1, and each subsequent number is the sum of the previous two. In mathematical terms, the sequence F_n of Fibonacci numbers is defined by the recurrence relation

$F_n = F_{n-1} + F_{n-2}$

with basic values

$F_0 = 0, \; F_1 = 1$

The sequence is named after Leonardo of Pisa, famous as Fibonacci.

FIFO list

This stands for **F**irst **I**n **F**irst **O**ut. This is used in algorithm of Queue.

File

A **computer file** is a block of arbitrary information, or resource for storing information, which is available to a computer program and is usually based on some kind of durable storage. A file is durable in the sense that it remains available for programs to use after the current program has finished. Computer files can be considered as the modern counterpart of paper documents which traditionally are kept in offices' and libraries' files, and this is the source of the term.

Filter

This is software programs designed to protect a computer system from harmful use like spam, virus. It also helps in protecting the machine from unreliable sources. They come in two main varieties: parental control filters, which block access to sites or categories of sites from a particular computer, and anti-virus filters, which prevent malicious software from infecting the protected computer. All organisations have their own filter. Different offices keep it to filter suspicious mails. Filters are must-haves for anyone with Internet access; they can prevent computer viruses from stealing personal information, and they can help parents keep inappropriate content away from kids.

Finite State Automaton

This is also known as Finite-State Machine (FSM) or simply a State Machine. It is mathematical model used to design computer programs and digital logic circuits. It is conceived as an abstract machine that can be in one of a finite number of *states*.

The machine is in only one state at a time. The state at any given time is called the "*current state*". The state can change from one state to another when triggering event or condition called *transition*. A particular FSM is defined by a list of the possible states. It can transition to and from each state with the triggering condition for each transition.

It can model a large number of problems, among which are electronic design automation, communication protocol design, parsing and other engineering applications. In biology and artificial intelligence research, state machines or hierarchies of state machines are sometimes used to describe neurological systems and in linguistics— to describe the grammars of natural languages

Firmware

This is a software often used to control various electronic devices. Examples of devices containing firmware range from end-user products such as remote controls or calculators, through computer parts and devices like hard disks, keyboards, TFT screens or memory cards. All the way to scientific instrumentation and industrial robotics Complex consumer devices, such as mobile phones, digital cameras, synthesizers, etc., contain firmware to enable the device's basic operation as well as implementing higher-level functions also use this.

But there are no strict boundaries between firmware and software because both are quite loose descriptive terms. The term *firmware* was originally coined in order to contrast to higher level software which could be changed without replacing a hardware component, and firmware is typically involved with very basic low-level operations without which a device would be completely non-functional.

This is also a relative term due to most embedded devices contain firmware at more than one level. Subsystems such as CPUs, flash chips, communication controllers, LCD modules, and so on, have their own program code and/or microcode, regarded as "part of the hardware" by the higher-level(s) firmware.

Low-level firmware resides in a ROM. While higher level firmware employs flash memory to allow for updates, at least in modern devices. Common reasons for updating firmware include fixing bugs or adding features to the device. Doing so usually involves loading a binary image file provided by the manufacturer into the device, according to a specific procedure; this is sometimes intended to be done by the end user.

First Generation

A computer from the earliest stage of computer development which ends in the early 1960s. It is characterized by the use of vacuum tubes. The performance of one operation at a time in strictly sequential fashion, and elementary software and usually including a program loader, simple utility routines, and an assembler to assist in program writing. The machine of this period was bulky in nature.

Flag

It can refer to one or more bits that are used to store a binary value or code which has assigned meaning, but can refer to uses of other data types. This is found as members of a defined data structure like database record. The meaning of the value contained in a flag will generally be defined in relation to the data structure it is part of. In many cases, the binary value of a flag will be understood to represent one of several possible states or statuses.

In other cases, the binary values may represent one or more attributes in a bit field, often related to abilities or permissions such as "can be written to" or "can be deleted". However, there are many other possible meanings that can be assigned to flag values. One common use of flags is to mark or designate data structures for future processing.

Flags are commonly used to control or indicate the intermediate or final state or outcome of different operations in microprocessors and other logic devices. The flags can be utilized in subsequent operations, such as in processing conditional jump instructions. For example a *je* (Jump if Equal) instruction in the X86 assembly language will result in a jump if the Z (zero) flag was set by some previous operation.

Floppy Disk

This is a storage medium composed of a disk of thin and flexible magnetic storage medium which is sealed in a rectangular plastic carrier lined with fabric that removes dust particles. They are read and written by a floppy disk drive. Initially this was 8-inch (200 mm) media and later came in 5.2 × 3.5-inch (133 mm) and 3.5-inch (89 mm) sizes. The contents stored in floppy are not secure. It may be lost, so it is not reliable way of storing the data. These day it is replaced by Compact Disc.

By 2010, computer motherboards were rarely manufactured with floppy drive support; 3 $^1/_2$" floppies could be used with an external USB drive, but 5 $^1/_4$", 8", and non-standard drives could only be handled by old equipment. While floppy disk drives still have some limited uses, especially with legacy industrial computer equipment, they have been superseded by data storage methods with much greater capacity, such as USB flash drives, portable external hard disk drives, optical discs, memory cards, and computer networks.

FM

This stands for Frequency Modulation which conveys information over a carrier wave by varying its instantaneous frequency. This contrasts with amplitude modulation in which the amplitude of the carrier is varied while its frequency remains constant. In analog applications, the difference between the instantaneous and the base frequency of the carrier is directly proportional to the instantaneous value of the input-signal amplitude.

Digital data can be sent by shifting the carrier's frequency among a range of settings, a technique known as frequency-shift keying. Frequency-shift keying is widely used in data and fax modems. FM modulation is also used in telemetry, radar, seismic prospecting and newborn EEG seizure monitoring. Frequency modulation is known as phase modulation when the carrier phase modulation is the time integral of the FM signal. FM is widely used for broadcasting music and speech, two-way radio systems, magnetic tape-recording systems and some video-transmission systems. In radio systems, frequency modulation with sufficient bandwidth provides an advantage in cancelling naturally-occurring noise.

Format

Formatting a disk involves testing the disk and writing a new file system onto the disk. In order for storage media, such as a hard drive or flash drive to be recognized by your computer, it first needs to be initialized, or "formatted." This enables the computer to read the disk's directory structure, which defines the way files and folders are organized on the disk.

You can use a disk utility program to format or reformat a disk. This will create a blank, empty disk for storing your files. Therefore, only format disks that don't contain important data or make sure you have backed up your data before reformatting a disk. At the time of formatting all present data were deleted. So keep backup of data before doing formatting.

Fragmentation

This refers to scattering of parts of a file throughout a disk, as when the operating system breaks up the file and fits it into the spaces left vacant by previously deleted files. Defragmentation software is present to solve these issues in personal computers.

Full adder

This adds binary numbers and gives values with carry out . A one-bit full adder adds three one-bit numbers, often written as *A*, *B*, and C_{in}. *A* and *B* are the operands while C_{in} is a bit carried in arises due to past addition. The circuit produces a two-bit output sum typically represented by the signals C_{out} and *S*. The one-bit full adder's truth table is:

Input			Output	
A	***B***	C_{in}	C_{out}	***S***
0	0	0	0	0
1	0	0	0	1
0	1	0	0	1
1	1	0	1	0
0	0	1	0	1
1	0	1	1	0
0	1	1	1	0
1	1	1	1	1

The Diagram of Full Adder is:

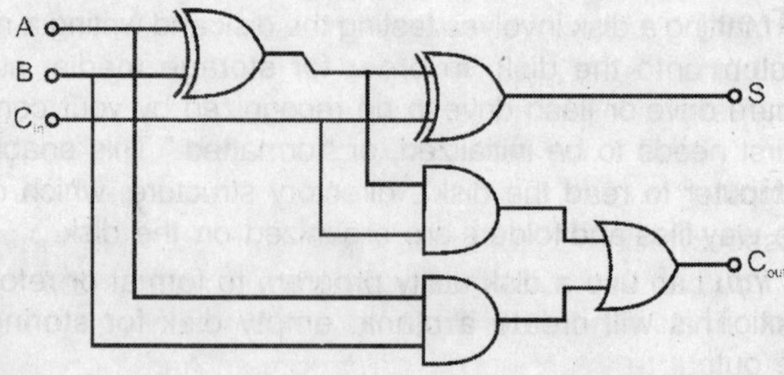

It can be implemented in many different ways such as with a custom transistor-level circuit or composed of other gates. One example of implementation is with,

$S = A \oplus B \oplus C_{in}$

$C_{out} = (A \cdot B) + (C_{in} \cdot (A \oplus B))$.

The final OR gate before the carry-out output may be replaced by an XOR gate without altering the resulting logic.

A full adder can be constructed from two half adders by connecting *A* and *B* to the input of one half adder, connecting the sum from that to an input to the second adder, connecting C_i to the other input and OR the two carry outputs. Equivalently, *S* could be made the three-bit XOR of *A*, *B*, and C_i, and C_{out} could be made the three-bit majority function of *A*, *B*, and C_i.

Full Duplex

This is sometimes refer to as *double-duplex* system. It allows communication in both directions, and, unlike half-duplex, allows this to happen simultaneously. Land-line telephone networks are example of full-duplex because they allow both callers to speak and be heard at the same time. A good analogy for a *full-duplex* system would be a two-lane road with one lane for each direction. The mobile phone is new example of this.

Full Tree

A full binary tree is a tree where all the leaf nodes are at the same level. No parent is without child.

Function

It associates one quantity, the *argument* also known as the *input*, with another quantity known as the *value* of the function, also known as the *output*. A function assigns exactly one output to each input. The argument and the value may be real numbers, but they can also be elements from any given set.

A function *f* with argument *x* is denoted *f*(*x*), which is read "*f* of *x*". An example of such a function is $f(x) = 3x$, the function which associates with every number *x* the number twice as large. For instance, if its argument is 3 its value is 6, and this is written $f(5) = 15$.

The input to a function can be any well defined object. For example, a function might associate the letter B with the number 1, the letter C with the number 2, and so on. There are many ways to describe or represent a function, such as a formula algorithm that computes the output for a given input, a graph that gives a picture of the function, or a table of values that gives the output for certain specified inputs. Tables of values are especially common in statistics, science, and engineering.

The set of all inputs to a particular function is called its domain. The set of all outputs of a particular function is called its image. Today it also has codomain. For every function, its codomain includes its image. For instance, a codomain of the function squaring real numbers $f(y) = y^2$ usually is defined to be the set of all real numbers. Codomain are useful for function composition. Composition $f \circ g$ (*g* followed by *f*) is defined if the codomain of *g* is the same as the domain of *f*. Thus the codomain of *g* defines what functions may follow *g*. The word range is used in some texts to refer to the image and in others to the codomain, in particular in computing it often refers to the codomain. The domain and codomain are often "understood." Thus for the example given above, $f(x) = 3x$, the domain and codomain were not stated explicitly. They might both be the set of all real numbers, but they might also be the set of integers. If the domain is the set of integers, then image consists of just the even integers.

Firewall

This is a device or set of devices or software designed to permit or deny network transmissions based upon a set of rules and is frequently used to protect networks from unauthorized access while permitting legitimate communications to pass.

Many personal computer operating systems include software-based firewalls to protect against threats from the public Internet. Many routers that pass data between networks contain firewall components and, conversely, many firewalls can perform basic routing functions. Offices are using this to block the unwanted websites to be accessed by employees.

FTP

It stands for File Transfer Protocol. It is a standard network protocol used to transfer files from one machine to another machine over a TCP-based network, such as the Internet. It is built on a client-server architecture and utilizes separate control and data connections between the client and server. FTP users may authenticate themselves using a clear-text sign-in protocol but can connect anonymously if the server is configured to allow it.

The first FTP client applications were interactive command-line tools, implementing standard commands and syntax. Graphical user interface clients have since been developed for many of the popular desktop operating systems in use today.

❑ ❑ ❑

Game Theory

This is a mathematical method for analyzing and calculating circumstances such as in games. It is the study of mathematical models of conflict and cooperation between intelligent rational decision-makers. Game theory is mainly used in economics, political science, and psychology, and other, more prescribed sciences, like logic and biology.

This first addressed zero-sum games so one person's gains exactly equals net losses of the other participants. In present scenario game theory applies to a wide range of class relations and developed into an umbrella term for the logical side of science, to include both human and non-humans, like computers.

Mathematical game theory had beginnings with some publications by Émile Borel. However, his results were limited, and the theory regarding the non-existence of blended-strategy equilibrium in two-player games was incorrect.

Modern game theory have mixed-strategy equilibrium in two-person zero-sum games and its proof by Neumann. This theory was developed extensively in the 1950s by many scholars. Game theory was later explicitly applied to biology in the 1970s, although similar developments go back at least as far as the 1930s.

Game theory has been widely recognized as an important tool in many fields. Eight game-theorists have won the Nobel Memorial Prize in Economic Sciences, and John Maynard Smith was awarded the Crafford Prize for his application of game theory to biology.

Garbage

It refers to objects, data, or other regions of the memory of a computer system or other system resources, which will not be used in any future computation by the system, or by a program running on it. Since computer systems have finite amounts of memory, it is frequently necessary to *deallocate* garbage and return it to the heap, or memory pool, so the underlying memory can be reused. Garbage is classified into two types:

- Semantic garbage: Semantic garbage is any object or data which will never be accessed by a running program, for any combination of inputs to the program.
- Syntactic garbage: Syntactic garbage refers to objects or data within a program's memory space that are *unreachable* from the program's root set.

The syntactic garbage is a subset of semantic garbage as it is entirely possible for an object to hold a reference to another object without the latter object being used.

Gateway

It is also called protocol converters and can operate at any network layer. It has the meanings like:

- It may contain devices such as protocol translators, impedance matching devices, rate converters, fault isolators, or signal translators as necessary to provide system interoperability. It also requires the establishment of mutually acceptable administrative procedures between both networks.

- A protocol translation/mapping gateway interconnects networks with different network protocol technologies by performing the required protocol conversions.

The activities of a gateway are more complex than that of the router or switch as it communicates using more than one protocol.

Grammar

It is a set of rules for for framing a formal language. A grammar does not describe the meaning of the strings. Its applications are found in science, theoretical, formal semantics, mathematical logic, and other areas.

A formal grammar is a set of rules for rewriting strings, along with a "start symbol" from which rewriting must start. So, a grammar is usually thought of as a language generator. However, it can also sometimes be used as the basis for a "recognizer"— a function in computing that determines whether a given string belongs to the language or is grammatically incorrect.

To describe such recognizers, formal language theory uses separate formalisms, known as automata theory. One of the interesting results of automata theory is that it is not possible to design a recognizer for certain formal languages. Parsing is the process of recognizing an utterance (a string in natural languages) by breaking it down to a set of symbols and analyzing each one against the grammar of the language. Most languages have the meanings of their utterances structured according to their syntax — a practice known as compositional semantics.

Gray Code

This is also known as Reflected Binary Code. The name is given after Gray. This is a binary numeral system where two successive values differ in only one bit. It is a non-weighted code. The reflected binary code was originally designed to prevent spurious output from electromechanical switches.

Today, Gray codes are widely used to facilitate error correction in data communications such as digital terrestrial television and cable TV systems. The issues with natural binary codes is that with real mechanical switches, it is very unlikely that switches will change states exactly in synchrony.

Dec	Gray	Binary
0	000	000
1	001	001
2	011	010
3	010	011
4	110	100
5	111	101
6	101	110
7	100	111

In the brief period while all are changing, the switches will read some spurious position. Even without key bounce, the transition might look like 001 — 100 — 010 — 001. If the output feeds into a sequential system (possibly via combinational logic) then the sequential system may store a false value.

The reflected binary code solves this problem by changing only one switch at a time, so there is never any ambiguity of position.

Gigabyte

This is a multiple unit byte for digital information storage. The prefix *giga* means 10^9 in the International System of Units (SI). So 1 *gigabyte* is 1000000000 bytes. It is represented by symbol **GB** or **Gbyte**, but not *Gb* (lower case *b*) which is typically used for the gigabit.

The term has also been used in some fields of computer science and information technology to denote the gibabyte, or 1073741824 (1024^3 or 2^{30}) bytes. The Institute of Electrical and Electronics Engineers (IEEE) defined the unit accordingly for the use in power switchgear In 2000, however, IEEE adopted the International Electro technical Commission (IEC) recommendation, which uses the metric prefix interpretation.

.gov

This indicates the government institution in web address.

Global Positioning System (GPS)

This is a space-based satellite navigation system that provides location and time information in all weathers and anywhere on or near the Earth: It also do action where there is an unobstructed line of sight to four or more GPS satellites. It is the property of the United States government and is freely accessible by anyone with a GPS receiver with some technical limitations which are only removed for military users. Other countries also had such systems like GLONAS of Russia, Galileo of UK etc. China and India also had such systems.

It provides critical capabilities to military, civil and commercial users around the world. It is an engine of economic growth and jobs, and has generated billions of dollars of economic activity. It maintains future war fighter advantage over opponents and is one of the four core military capabilities. In addition, GPS is the backbone for modernizing the global air traffic system.

The GPS project was developed in 1973 to overcome the limitations of previous navigation systems. GPS was created and realized by the U.S. Department of Defence and was originally run with 24 satellites. It became fully operational in 1994.

Advances in technology and new demands on the existing system have now led to efforts to modernize the GPS system and implement the next generation of GPS III satellites and Next Generation Operational Control System (OCX). In addition to GPS, other systems are in use or under development.

Graphics

This is a sub-field of computer science which studies methods for digitally synthesizing and manipulating visual content. Although the term often refers to the study of three-dimensional computer graphics, it also encompasses two-dimensional graphics and processing. It enhances the picture quality of computer and other devices. It is mostly required in gaming system.

Georgian Calendar

This is also known as the Western calendar, or Christian calendar. This is the internationally accepted civil calendar. It was introduced by Pope Gregory XIII and the calendar was named, by a decree signed on 24 February 1582. The reformed calendar was adopted later that year by a handful of countries, with other countries adopting it over the following centuries.

The motivation for the Gregorian reform was that the Julian calendar assumes that the time between vernal equinoxes is 365.25 days, when in fact it is presently almost exactly 11 minutes shorter. The error between these values accumulated at the rate of about three days every four centuries, resulting in the equinox occurring on March 11 and moving steadily earlier in the Julian calendar at the time of the Gregorian reform. Since the Spring equinox was tied to the celebration of Easter, the Roman Catholic Church considered that this e.g. steady movement in the date of the equinox was undesirable.

It contained two parts, a reform of the Julian calendar as used up to Pope Gregory's time, together with a reform of the lunar cycle used by the Church along with the Julian calendar for calculating dates of Easter. Lilius' proposal included reducing the number of leap years in four centuries from 100 to 97, by making 3 out of 4 centurial years common instead of leap years.

Groupware

This is computer software designed to help people involved in a common task to achieve goals. This is also known as collaborative software. The design intent of collaborative software (groupware) is to transform the way documents and rich media is shared to enable more effective team collaboration. Collaboration, with respect to information technology, seems to have several definitions. Some are defensible but others are so broad they lose meaningful application. Understanding the differences in human interactions is necessary to ensure that appropriate technologies are employed to meet interaction needs.

It requires individuals working together in a coordinated fashion, towards a common goal. Accomplishing the goal is the primary purpose for bringing the team together. Collaborative software helps facilitate action-oriented teams working together over geographic distances by providing tools that aid communication, collaboration and the process of problem solving. Additionally, collaborative software may support project management functions, such as task assignments, time-managing deadlines, and shared calendars. The artefacts, the tangible evidence of the problem solving process, and the final outcome of the collaborative effort, require documentation and may involve archiving project plans, deadlines and deliverables.

GUI

It stands for **G**raphical **U**ser **I**nterface. It is a type of user interface that allows users to interacts with electronic devices like computer with images rather than text commands. It can be used in computers, devices such as MP3 players, portable media players or gaming devices, household appliances and office equipment. It represents the information and actions available to a user through graphical icons and visual indicators such as secondary notation, as opposed to text-based interfaces, typed command labels or text navigation. The actions are usually performed through direct manipulation of the graphical elements. It simplified the handling of electronics devices.

There are several tools available in market to form GUI while developing the software.

❑ ❑ ❑

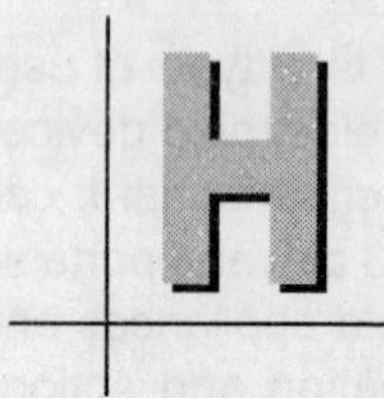

Hacker

They break into computers and computer networks security. They illegally use the information stored in database or personal computer. The process of stealing the data is known as hacking like — cracking password, stealing bank account information etc. According to some shrewd hackers, it is an art rather than crime.

They may be motivated by a multitude of reasons, including profit, protest, or challenge. While other uses of the word hacker exist that are not related to computer security rather than they are rarely used in mainstream context. They are subject to the long standing hacker definition controversy about the true meaning of the term hacker. The term hacker is reclaimed by computer programmers who argue that someone breaking into computers is better called a cracker, not making a difference between computer criminals (black hats) and computer security experts (white hats).

They break the security code. This is a crime. Governments around the world have framed cyber laws to tackle the problems of security.

Half Adder

This is a type of Adder and adds two one-bit binary numbers. The half-adder adds the two numbers A and B to produce the sum digit S and the carry digit c (see Table).

The "Adder" is an arithmetic component of digital computer. It is used for adding arithmetic digits. It takes input as binary number. The digits in the units digit place in the addends are added first when decimal numbers are added digit by digit. But If the result is a two-digit number, only the digit in the unit's place of this number is entered in the unit's place of the sum; the tens are carried — that is, the digit in the tens place is added to the digits in the ten's places of the original addends. The addition operation is then carried out on the ten's digits. Same process is continuously repeated for the higher order digits until the final sum is obtained. The half-adder design is as:

Inputs and Outputs of a Half-adder

Inputs		*Outputs*	
x	***y***	***S***	***c***
0	0	0	0
1	0	1	0
0	1	1	0
1	1	0	1

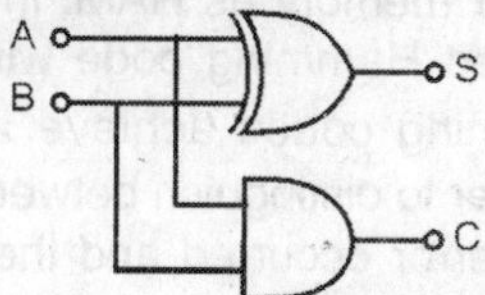

It incorporates an XOR gate for *S* and an AND gate for *C*. Half adders cannot be used compositely, given their incapacity for a carry-in bit.

Hamiltonian Path

This is also called Traceable Path. This is a path in an undirected graph which visits each vertex exactly once. The Hamiltonian cycle is moving in an undirected graph and visits each vertex exactly once and returns to the starting vertex. The naming of Hamiltonian Path or cycle occurred on the name of William Rowan Hamilton who invented the Icosian game (also known as Hamilton's puzzle today).

Hamilton solved this problem using the Icosian Calculus, an algebraic structure based on roots of unity with many similarities to the quaternions (also invented by Hamilton). This solution does not generalize to arbitrary graphs. However, despite being named after Hamilton, Hamiltonian cycles in polyhedra had also been studied a year earlier by Thomas Kirkman.

Hamming Code

This belongs to family of codes. It generalize the Hamming (7,4)-code invented by Richard Hamming in 1950. It can detect up to two and correct up to one bit errors. The general parity code can detect only an odd number of errors and cannot correct errors. This is perfect code because it achieve the highest possible rate for codes with their block length and minimum distance 3.

Due to the simplicity of Hamming codes, they are widely used in computer memory as RAM. In this context, one often uses an extended Hamming code with one extra parity bit. Extended Hamming codes achieve a distance of 4, which allows the decoder to distinguish between the situation in which at most one bit error occurred and the situation in which two bit errors occurred. In this sense, extended Hamming codes are single-error correcting and double-error detecting, and often referred to as SECDED.

Handshaking

It is usually a process when a computer is about to communicate with a foreign device to establish rules for communication. When a computer communicates with another device like a modem, printer, or network server, it needs to handshake with it to establish a connection. It makes it possible to connect relatively heterogeneous equipment over a communication channel without the need for human intervention to set parameters. The example of handshaking is of modems, which typically negotiate communication parameters for a brief period when a connection is first established, and thereafter use those parameters to provide optimal information transfer over the channel as a function of its quality and capacity.

This is an automated process of negotiation which sets parameters of a communications channel established between two entities before normal communication over the channel begins. It follows the physical establishment of the channel and precedes normal information transfer. Handshaking can be used to negotiate parameters that are acceptable to equipment and systems at both ends of the communication channel, including, but not limited to, information transfer rate, coding alphabet, parity, interrupt procedure, and other protocol or hardware features. Handshaking is technique of communication between two entities.

Hardware

The Computer had two parts known as Software and Hardware. Software is programme like operating system, system software, application software etc. Which makes computer live. On the other side hardware is its electronic component like motherboard, hard disk, CPU, CD–ROM etc.

The hardware are manufactured by different electronic instruments like chip, IC, resistor, diode capacitor etc.

Hashing

This is a way of searching data or information from the database. This is one of the most important way of searching algorithm which maps large data sets, called keys into smaller data sets. The values returned by a hash function are called hash values, hash codes, hash sums, checksums or simply hashes.

This is mostly used to accelerate table lookup or data comparison tasks such as finding items in a database, detecting duplicated or similar records in a large file, finding similar stretches in DNA sequences, and so on.

This is a contract in many programming languages that allow the user to override equality and hash functions for an object, that if two objects are equal, their hash codes must be the same. This is important in order for it to be possible to find an element in a hash table quickly since two of the same element would both hash to the same slot.

Hash Table

This is also known as Hash Map. It keeps hash values creating during Hashing. This is a data structure that uses a hash function to map identifying values, known as keys (e.g., a name), to their associated values (e.g., age sex, their telephone number). Thus, a hash table implements an associative array. The hash function is used to transform the key into the index (the *hash*) of an array element (the *slot* or *bucket*) where the corresponding value is to be sought.

It should map each possible key to a unique slot index, but this ideal is rarely achievable in practice. Unless the hash keys are fixed, the new entries are never added to the table after it is created.

Heap Sort

This is an algorithm of sorting the data in data structure. This is a comparison-based sorting algorithm to create a sorted array or list. This is part of the selection sort family. But it had demerits that slower in practice on most machines than a well implemented quick sort. But it has an advantage of a more favourable worst-case O(n log n) runtime.

It begins by building a heap out of the data set, and then removing the largest item and placing it at the end of the partially sorted array. After removing the largest item, it reconstructs the heap, removes the largest remaining item, and places it in the next open position from the end of the partially sorted array. This is repeated until there are no items left in the heap and the sorted array is full. Elementary implementations require two arrays — one to hold the heap and the other to hold the sorted elements.

It inserts the input list elements into a binary heap data structure. The largest value or the smallest value are extracted until none remain, the values having been extracted in sorted order. The heap's invariant is preserved after each extraction, so the only cost is that of extraction.

Hexadecimal Number

This is also known as base 16, or hex number. This is a way of representing the number system. This is a positional numeral system with a radix or base 16. It uses sixteen distinct symbols ranging 0–9 to represent values zero to nine, and A, B, C, D, E, F to represent values ten to fifteen. For example, the hexadecimal number
2BC3 is equal in decimal to :
$(2 \times 16^3) + (11 \times 16^2) + (12 \times 16^1) + (3 \times 16^0)$

Each hexadecimal digit represents four binary digits (bits) (also called a "nibble"), and the primary use of hexadecimal notation is as a human-friendly representation of binary-coded values in computing and digital electronics. For example, byte values can range from 0 to 255 (decimal) but may be more conveniently represented as two hexadecimal digits in the range 00 through FF. Hexadecimal is also commonly used to represent computer memory addresses.

High Level Language

This is a programming language having strong abstraction from the details of the computer. It is programmers language.

Compilers and Interpreters are used as to convert the Low level language to High level languages and high level to low level languages.

In comparison to low-level programming languages, it may use natural language elements, be easier to use or be from the specification of the program, making the process of developing a program simpler and more understandable with respect to a low-level language. The amount of abstraction provided defines how "high-level" a programming language is.

The first high-level programming language to be designed for a computer was Plankalkül, created by Konrad Zuse. However, it was not implemented in his time, and his original contributions were isolated from other developments.

Computer or high definition machines always keep information in low level language.

Histogram

It is a graphical representation showing the distribution of data. It is a probability distribution of a continuous variable. This was first introduced by Karl Pearson. A histogram consists of tabular frequencies, shown as adjacent rectangles, erected over discrete intervals (bins), with an area equal to the frequency of the observations in the interval. The height of a rectangle is also equal to the frequency density of the interval, i.e., the frequency divided by the width of the interval. The total area of the histogram is equal to the number of data.

There are several methods for histogram like circular, Pie Chart. It may also have normalized displaying relative frequencies. It then shows the proportion of cases that fall into each of several categories, with the total area equaling 1. The categories are usually specified as consecutive, non-overlapping intervals of a variable. The intervals must be adjacent, and often are chosen to be of the same size.

Homomorphism

This is a structure-preserving map between two algebraic structures like groups, rings, or vector spaces. The word homomorphism comes from the Greek language— homo*s* meaning "same" and morph*e* meaning "shape".

Hybrid Computer

These are computers which exhibit features of analog computers as well as digital computers. The digital component normally serves as the controller and provides logical operations, while the analog component normally serves as a solver of differential equations.

The Analog computers are fast because they can solve most complex equations at the rate at which a signal traverses the circuit, which is generally an appreciable fraction of the speed of light. On the other hand, the precision of analog computers is not good; they are limited to three, or at most, four digits of precision.

On the other hand, Digital computers can take the solution of equations to almost unlimited precision. But these are quite slow compared to analog computers. The complex equations are approximated using iterative numerical methods which take huge numbers of iterations, depending on how good the initial "guess" at the final value is and how much precision is desired. For many real-time operations, the speed of such *digital* calculations is too slow to be of much use like very high frequency phased array radars or for weather calculations or space technology.

It can be used to obtain a very good but relatively imprecise 'base' value, using an analog computer front-end, which is then fed into a digital computer iterative process to achieve the final desired degree of precision. With a three or four digit, highly accurate numerical base, the total digital computation time necessary to reach the desired precision is dramatically reduced, since many fewer iterations are required.

One of the main technical problems to be overcome in hybrid computers is minimizing digital-computer noise in analog computing elements and ground systems.

Hanging

This indicates suspension of work by any machine like computer, gazette etc. According to *Oxford English Dictionary* hanging in this sense is "specifically to put to death by suspension by the neck", though it formerly also referred to crucifixion and death by impalement in which the body would remain "hanging".

It oneself describes a method of suicide in which a person applies a ligature to the neck and brings about unconsciousness and then death, by means of partial suspension or partial weight-bearing on the ligature. This method has been most often used in prisons or other institutions, where full suspension support is difficult to devise.

It occurs due to several reasons :

- Access of big memory disk.
- Network congestion.
- Issuing several applications at a time.

Host Computer

This is the base computer in data communication through which all computers are linked. Computers participating in networks that use the Internet Protocol may also be called IP hosts. Specifically, computers participating in the Internet are called *Internet hosts*, sometimes Internet nodes. Internet hosts and other IP hosts have one or more IP addresses assigned to their network interfaces. The addresses are configured either manually by an administrator, automatically at start-up by means of the Dynamic Host Configuration

Protocol (DHCP), or by stateless address auto configuration methods.

A network host is a computer connected to a computer network. A network host may offer information resources, services, and applications to users or other nodes on the network. A network host is a network node that is assigned a network layer host address.

Hub

It is an electronics device used to connect different machines in a network. It is used in a wired network to connect cables from a number of devices together. The hub allows each device to talk to the others. Hubs aren't used in networks with only wireless connections because network devices such as routers and adapters communicate directly with one another. Hubs are such simple devices that they require no configuration, and have no manuals. Their function is now included in other devices such as routers and modems. If you require a stand-alone appliance, use a switch instead. Switches provide better performance and features than hubs.

HDTV

This stands for High Definition Television. This is latest invention. The picture quality of this is high and better than other TVs.

Home Page

It has various related meanings to do with web sites:

- It refers to the initial or main web page of a web site called the **front page.**
- The web page or local file that automatically loads when a web browser starts or when the browser's "home" button is pressed; this is also called a **start page**. The user

can specify the URL of the page to be loaded, or alternatively choose e.g., to re-load the most recent web page browsed.

- A personal web page, for example, at a web hosting service or a university web site, that typically is stored in the home directory of the user.

Any web page can be made home page by doing specific setting in web browser.

HTML

This stands for Hyper Text Markup Language. Different web pages are designed with the help of this. It is the predominant mark-up language for web pages. This is the basic building-blocks of Web Pages.

HTML is written in the form of HTML elements consisting of *tags*, enclosed in angle brackets (<html>) within the web page content. The tags commonly come in pairs like <h1> and </h1>. While some tags known as empty elements are unpaired for example<img>. The first tag in a pair is the *start tag*, the second tag is the *end tag*. In between these tags web designers can add text, tags, comments and other types of text-based content.

The purpose of a web browser is to read HTML documents and compose them into visible or audible web pages. The browser does not display the HTML tags, but uses the tags to interpret the content of the page.

It forms the building blocks of all websites and allows images and objects to be embedded and can be used to create interactive forms. It provides a means to create structured documents by denoting structural semantics for text such as headings, paragraphs, lists, links, quotes and other items. It can embed scripts in languages such as Java Script which affect the behaviour of HTML webpages.

HTTP

This stands for Hypertext Transfer Protocol. This indicates rules and regulations to do communication between two machines. It is a networking protocol for distributed, collaborative, hypermedia information systems. It is the basic of data communication for the World Wide Web.The standard development of HTTP has been coordinated by the Internet Engineering Task Force (IETF) and the World Wide Web Consortium (W3C), culminating in the publication of a series of Requests for Comments (RFCs), most notably RFC 2616 (June 1999), which defines HTTP/1.1, the version of HTTP in common use.

Huffman Coding

The term refers to the use of a variable-length code table for encoding a source code where the variable-length code table has been derived in a particular way based on the estimated probability of occurrence for each possible value of the source code. This is an encoding algorithm used for lossless data compression. It was developed by David A. Huffman. It gets name on its inventor.

It uses a specific method for choosing the representation for each symbol, resulting in a code. It expresses the most common source symbols using shorter strings of bits than are used for less common source symbols. Huffman was able to design the most efficient compression method *of this type*: no other mapping of individual source symbols to unique strings of bits will produce a smaller average output size when the actual symbol frequencies agree with those used to create the code.

Hyperlink

This is a reference to data that the reader can directly follow. When someone click this, it leads to specific action or address. A hyperlink points to a whole document or to a specific element within a document. Hypertext is text with hyperlinks. A software system for viewing and creating hypertext is a *hypertext system*, and to create a hyperlink is *to hyperlink* (or simply *to link*). A user following hyperlinks is said to *navigate* or *browse* the hypertext.

The document containing a hyperlink is known as its **source** document to web pages. A hyperlink has an *anchor*, which is the location within a document from which the hyperlink can be followed. For example, in an online reference work such as Wikipedia, many words and terms in the text are hyperlinked to definitions of those terms. Hyperlinks are often used to implement reference mechanisms, such as tables of contents, footnotes, bibliographies, indexes, letters and glossaries.

It reduces the searching time of user because it directly goes to the specific location by clicking this.

❑❑❑

I

Idempotence

These are certain operations in computer science that can be applied multiple times without changing the result beyond the initial application. The idea of idempotence arises in a number of places in abstract algebra particularly in the theory of projectors and closure operators and in functional programming which is connected to the property of referential transparency.

Idea was introduced by Benjamin Peirce. He invented this in the context of elements of an algebra that remain invariant when raised to a positive integer power. It literally means the same power.

Depending on the concept there are several meanings of idempotence like:

- A unary operation or function is idempotent if-,whenever it is applied twice or thrice to any value, it gives same result as it were applied first. For example, the value: abs(abs(y)) = abs(y).
- A binary operation is idempotent if, whenever it is applied to two equal values, it gives that value as the result. For example, the operation giving the maximum value of two values is idempotent: max(y, y) = y.
- Given a binary operation, an idempotent element for the operation is a value for which the operation, when given

that value for both of its operands, gives the value as the result. For example, the number 0 is an idempotent of multiplication: 0 × 0 = 0.

Identity matrix

This is also known as unit matrix. The size *n* is the *n*×*n* square matrix with ones on the main diagonal and zeros elsewhere is Identity Matrix. It is denoted by I_n, or simply by I (If the size is immaterial or can be trivially determined by the context). In some fields, such as quantum mechanics, the identity matrix is denoted by a boldface one, 1.

For example,

$$I_1=[1],\ I_2=\begin{bmatrix}1 & 0\\ 0 & 1\end{bmatrix},\ I_3=\begin{bmatrix}1 & 0 & 0\\ 0 & 1 & 0\\ 0 & 0 & 1\end{bmatrix},\ldots,\begin{bmatrix}1 & 0 & \cdots & 0\\ 0 & 1 & \cdots & 0\\ \vdots & \vdots & \ddots & \vdots\\ 0 & 0 & \cdots & 1\end{bmatrix}$$

IEEE

This stands for Institute of Electrical and Electronics Engineers. It describes itself as "the world's largest technical professional society — promoting the development and application of electrical technology and allied sciences for the benefit of humanity, the advancement of the profession, and the well-being of our members. "The IEEE fosters the development of standards that often become national and international standards." The organization publishes a number of journals, has many local chapters, and several large societies in special areas, such as the IEEE Computer Society.

Incremental Compiler

This is type of compiler that can compile partial programs, and can compile additional statements for a program without recompiling the whole program. Incremental compilers were at one time in vogue for interactive programming, but interactive language systems nowadays are almost always implemented in an interpretive manner.

They converts low level programming language to high level programming language i.e., binary code.

Index Register

This is a processor register used for modifying operand addresses during the run of a program for doing vector/array operations in Central Processing Unit. It was first used in 1949 in the British Manchester Mark 1 computer.

This is used for indirect addressing where an *immediate* constant is added to the contents of a register to form the address to the actual operand or data. Some instruction sets allow more than one index register to be used in that case an additional instruction field specifies the second index register to use.

Information Technology

IT is concerned with technology to handle digital information. It serves with several electronics equipment and software programmes. The acquisition, processing, storage and dissemination of vocal, pictorial, textual and numerical information by a microelectronics-based combination of computing and telecommunications are its main fields.

In modern sense, first appeared in 1958 article published in the Harvard Business Review; the authors Leavitt and Whisler commented that "the new technology does not yet have a single established name. We shall call it information technology (IT)." Some of the modern and emerging fields of Information technology are next generation web technologies, bioinformatics, cloud computing, global information systems, large scale knowledge bases, etc. Advancements are mainly driven in the field of computer science.

This is the backbone of modern civilisation. Today world are roaming with 4G and 5G technology. IT minimised the gap between different continents.

Initialisation

It is a process of initiating defined values for variable data that is used by a computer program. Differnt programming languages have different initialisation process. Geneally, it is used to start any application with some initial value. For example, an operating system or application program is installed with default or user-specified values that determine certain aspects of how the system or program is to function. Typically, these values are stored in initialization. When the operating system or an application program is first loaded into memory, a part of the program performs initialization — that is, it looks in the initialization files, finds definite values to substitute for variable values, and acts accordingly. For example, the desktop appearance and application programs that are to be started along with the operating system are identified and loaded.

Integrated Circuit (IC)

This is also known as monolithic integrated circuit. This is an electronic circuit manufactured by the patterned diffusion of trace elements into the surface of a thin substrate of semiconductor material. There are several types of electronics devices mounted on circuit like capacitor, resistor, diode etc. Additional materials are deposited and patterned to form interconnections between semiconductor devices.

Today, these are used in virtually all electronic equipments and have revolutionized the world of electronics. Computers, mobile phones, and other digital appliances are now inextricable parts of the structure of modern societies, made possible by the low cost of production of integrated circuits.

Interface

In programming language, Interfaces are used to define classes which do not have body.

In hardware term, this is a boundary across which two independent systems meet and act on or communicate with each other. In computer technology, there are several types of interfaces. User interface – the keyboard, mouse, menus of a computer system. The user interface allows the user to communicate with the operating system.

Internet Protocol

This is represented as IP and are principal communications protocol used for relaying datagram (packets) across an internetwork using the Internet Protocol Suite. It is the primary protocol that establishes the Internet.

IP is the protocol used in the Internet Layer of the Internet Protocol Suite and has the task of delivering datagram from the source host to the destination host solely based on their addresses. IP defines addressing methods and structures for datagram encapsulation.

ISDN

This stands for **I**ntegrated **S**ervices **D**igital **N**etwork. This is a set of communications standards for simultaneous digital transmission of voice, video, data, and other network services over the traditional circuits of the public switched telephone network. It was first framed in 1988. Prior to ISDN, the telephone system was viewed as a way to transport voice, with some special services available for data. The key feature of ISDN is that it integrates speech and data on the same lines, adding features that were not available in the classic telephone system. There are several kinds of access interfaces to ISDN defined as Basic Rate Interface (BRI), Primary Rate Interface (PRI) and Broadband ISDN (B-ISDN).

ISO

It stands for **I**nternational **O**rganization for **S**tandardization and is the world's largest developer and publisher of International Standards. It is a network of the national standards institutes of 162 countries with Central Secretariat at Geneva, Switzerland. It is a non-governmental organization that forms a bridge between the public and private sectors. On the one hand, many of its member institutes are part of the governmental structure of their countries, or are mandated by their government. On the other hand, other members have their roots uniquely in the private sector, having been set up by national partnerships of industry associations.

Isomorphism

This is mapping between objects which shows a relationship between two operations. When exists an isomorphism between two structures they called isomorphic structures. In certain cases, isomorphic structures are structurally identical.

An isomorphism is a bijective map f such that both f and its inverse f^{-1} are structure-preserving maps between two algebraic structures.

So isomorphism refers as $f : X \to Y$ in a category for which there exists an "inverse" $f^{-1}: Y \to X$, with the property that both $f^{-1} f = id_X$ and $f f^{-1} = id_Y$.

Infinite Loop

This is also known as endless loop having a sequence of instructions in a computer program which endlessly run, either due to the loop having no terminating condition or having one that can never be met. Other reasons are causes the loop to start over.

In earlier operating systems with cooperative multitasking infinite loops normally caused the entire system to become unresponsive. With the now-prevalent pre-emptive multitasking model, infinite loops usually cause the program to consume all available processor time, but can usually be terminated by the user. Busy-wait loops are also sometimes misleadingly called "infinite loops". One possible cause of a computer "freezing" is an infinite loop; others include deadlock and access violations.

Inheretance

This is a technique to suggest an object to inherit characteristics from another object. In more concrete terms, an object is able to pass on its state and behaviours to its children. For inheritance to work the objects need to have characteristics in common with each other. This is frequently used in Java and C++ programming language.

Intellectual Property Right

This is related to software, copy right, patent etc. This refers to a number of distinct types of creations of the mind for which a set of exclusive rights are recognized—and the corresponding fields of law. To handle the Intellectual Property government has framed intellectual property laws in which owners are granted certain exclusive rights to a variety of intangible assets, such as musical, literary, and artistic works; discoveries and inventions; and words, phrases, symbols, and designs. Common types of intellectual property rights include copyrights, trademarks, patents, industrial design rights and trade secrets in some jurisdictions.

Internet

This is a global system of interconnected computers and computer networks that use the standard Internet protocol suite (TCP/IP) to serve billions of users worldwide. It is a *network of networks* that consists of millions of private, public, academic, business, and government networks, of local to global scope. These are linked by a broad array of electronic, wireless and optical networking technologies. The Internet carries a vast range of information resources and services, such as the inter-linked hypertext documents of the World Wide Web(WWW) and the infrastructure to support email.

This reduces the continental distances between different continents. It revolutionise the world and give it glocal shape. glocal stands for global plus local. Social networking sites which are most popular today are pats of internet. Google stands as a big entrepreneur of the world due to internet.

Intranet

The term refers only to the organization's internal website. This is also computer network that uses Internet Protocol technology to securely share any part of an organization's information or network operating system but within the organization. This is used in contrast to *internet*, a network between organizations, and instead refers to a network within an organization.

It may host multiple private websites and constitute an important component and focal point of internal communication and collaboration. Any of the well known Internet protocols may be found in an intranet, such as HTTP (web services), SMTP (e-mail), and FTP (file transfer protocol). Internet technologies are often deployed to provide modern interfaces to legacy information systems hosting corporate data.

IP Tunnelling

This is an Internet Protocol network communications channel between two networks. It is used to transport another network protocol by encapsulation of its packets. It is used to connect to server by back gate. In conjunction with the IP protocol they may be used to create a virtual private network between two or more private networks across a public network such as the Internet. There are several tools for IP tunnelling.

This is often used for connecting two disjoint IP networks which don't have a native routing path to each other. It is connected as underlying routable protocol across an intermediate transport network. Another prominent use is to connect islands of IPv6 installations across the IPv4 Internet. The connection looks like,

IP header	→	Outer IP header
IP payload		Tunnel headers
		Inner IP header
		IP payload

In IP tunnelling, every IP packet, including addressing information of its source and destination IP networks, is encapsulated within another packet format native to the transit network.

i-RAM

This is a solid-state Random Access Memory produced by Gigabyte which has four DIMM slots to allow Personnel Computer's DDR RAM to be used to store data.

It connects via a SATA port. The i-RAM is bottlenecked by the SATA interface, which limits bandwidth to a maximum sustained throughput of 150 MB/s. This speed limitation is offset by near instant access, with latency results of 0.1 ms recorded.

IP Address

This is also known as the “host number” or “host address.”This is the IP address that described the details of any machine location and registration. The identifier of the network is known as “network number” while the identifier of the device is as “machine address”. Security agencies catches the fraud entail activities through the Machine Address like who send any threatening mail, did unauthorised use of any banking credential etc. This is unique for each machine.

❑❑❑

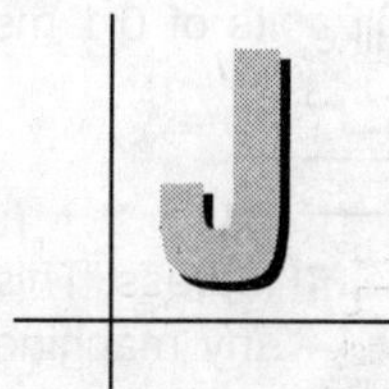

JK Flip-flop

This is a type of Flip- Flop augmenting the behaviour of the SR flip-flop by interpreting the S = R = 1 condition as a "flip" or toggle command. Specifically the combination J = 0, K = 1 is a command to reset the flip-flop while the combination J = K = 1 is a command to toggle the flip-flop. Toggle means change its output to the logical complement of its current value.

The JK flip-flop is therefore a universal flip-flop which configured to work as an SR flip-flop, a D flip-flop, or a T flip-flop.

The equation of the JK flip-flop is:

$$Q_{next} = J\bar{Q} + \bar{K}Q$$

While truth table is:

JK FLIP FLOP OPERATION								
Characteristic table				***Excitation table***				
J	***K***	Q_{next}	**Comment**	***Q***	Q_{next}	***J***	***K***	**Comment**
0	0	Q	hold state	0	0	0	X	No change
0	1	0	reset	0	1	1	X	Set
1	0	1	set	1	0	X	1	Reset
1	1	Q	toggle	1	1	X	0	No change

The J-K Flip-Flop can be represented as:

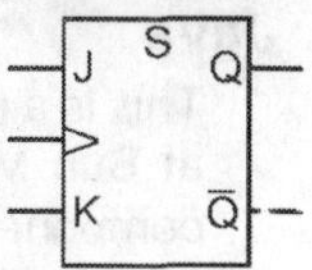

The electronics pulses of J-K Flip-Flop is like,

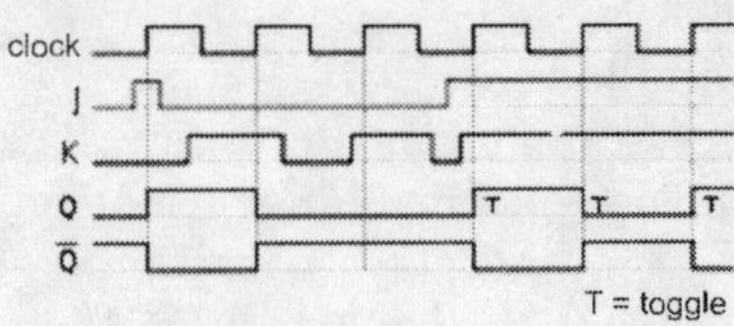

Jack

This is system for handling real-time and low latency audio signal. It runs on Linux, Solaris, FreeBSD, OS X and Windows and can be ported to other POSIX-conformant platforms. It can connect a number of different applications to an audio device, as well as allowing them to share audio between themselves. Its clients can run in their own processes (i.e. as normal applications), or can they can run within the JACK server .JACK also has support for distributing audio processing across a network, both fast & reliable LANs as well as slower, less reliable WANs.

Junk Mail

This is also known as spam email or unsolicited bulk email. They are harmful for the local machine. They may be virus. It is a subset of spam that involves nearly identical messages sent to numerous recipients by email. Definitions of spam usually include the aspects that email is unsolicited and sent in bulk. The opposite of "spam", email which one wants, is called "ham", usually when referring to a message's automated analysis such as Bayesian filtering.

Java

This is a programming language developed by James Gosling at Sun Microsystems and released in 1995. This is a core component of Sun Microsystems' Java platform. This is object oriented language. The language derives much of its syntax from C and C++ but has a simpler object model and fewer low-level facilities.

Java applications are typically compiled to byte code (class file) that can run on any Java Virtual Machine (JVM) regardless of computer architecture. Java is a general-purpose, concurrent, class-based programme specifically designed to have as few implementation dependencies as possible. It is intended to let application developers "write once, run anywhere."

Almost 60 percent software professional depend upon java. Java is currently one of the most popular programming languages in use particularly for client-server web applications. The idea was "write once, run anywhere" means that any program written in Java can be run on any machine. Java is not OS dependent, which makes it very portable from smart phones to different OS computers.

Java Script

Java Script is primarily used in the form of client-side Java Script, implemented as part of a Web browser in order to provide enhanced user interfaces and dynamic websites. This enables programmatic access to computational objects within a host environment.

This is a prototype-based scripting language that is dynamic, weakly typed and has first-class functions. It is a multi-paradigm language, supporting object-oriented and functional programming styles.

Java Script's use in applications outside Web pages — for example in PDF documents, site-specific browsers, and desktop widgets — is also significant. Newer and faster Java Script VMs and frameworks built upon them have also increased the popularity of Java Script for server-side web applications.

JVM

This stands for **J**ava **V**irtual **M**achine. This is a software that is implemented on non-virtual hardware and on standard operating systems. It provides an environment where Java byte code can be executed. It enables automatic exception handling which provides root-cause.

This is distributed along with a set of standard class libraries that implement the Java application programming interface (API). Appropriate APIs bundled together with JVM and form the Java Runtime Environment (JRE).

It is available for many hardware and software platforms. The use of the same byte code for all JVMs on all platforms allows Java to be described as a "write once, run anywhere" programming language, as opposed to "write once, compile anywhere", which describes .cross-platform compiled languages. Thus, the JVM is a crucial component of the Java platform.

JDBC

This stands for **J**ava **D**ata **B**ase **C**onnector. This is a software component enabling a Java application to interact with a database. The drivers are analogous to ODBC drivers. To connect with individual databases, JDBC (the Java Database Connectivity API) requires drivers for each database. The JDBC driver gives out the connection to the database and implements the protocol for transferring the query and result between client and database. JDBC technology drivers fit into one of four categories.

JPEG

This stands for **J**oint **P**hotographic **E**xperts **G**roup and commonly used method of lossy compression for digital image. This is way of making picture. The degree of compression can be adjusted, allowing a selectable trade-off between storage size and image quality. It achieves 10:1 compression with little perceptible loss in image quality.

The compression is used in a number of image file formats. This is the most common image format used by digital cameras and other photographic image capture devices. It is the most common format for storing and transmitting photographic images on the World Wide Web. These format variations are often not distinguished, and are simply called JPEG.

❑ ❑ ❑

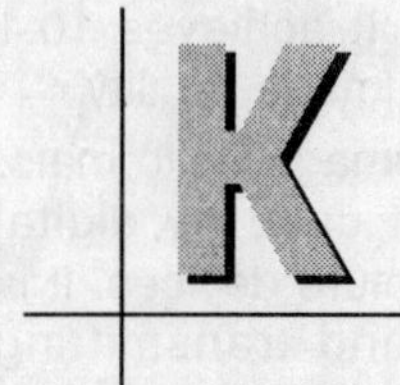

Karnaugh Map

This is denoted as K-map. This is a method to simplify Boolean algebraic expressions and was developed by Maurice Karnaugh in 1953.On the name of inventor, it is known as Karnaugh Map. It reduces the need for extensive calculations by taking advantage of humans' pattern-recognition capability and permitting the rapid identification and elimination of potential race conditions.

It is represented into rectangular fashion as binary digits in the map represent the function's output for any given combination of inputs. So '0' is written in the upper leftmost corner of the map because $f = 0$ when $A = 0$, $B = 0$, $C = 0$, $D = 0$. Similarly we mark the bottom right corner as '1' because $A = 1$, $B = 0$, $C = 1$, $D = 0$ gives $f = 1$. Note that the values are ordered in a Gray code, so that precisely one variable changes between any pair of adjacent cells.

The Boolean variables are transferred generally from a truth table and ordered according to the principles of Gray code in which only one variable changes in between adjacent squares is desirable. Once the table is generated and the output possibilities are transcribed, the data is arranged into the largest possible groups containing 2^n cells (n = 0, 1, 2, 3...). The mid-term is generated through the axiom laws of Boolean algebra. The following is an unsimplified Boolean Algebra function with Boolean variables *A*, *B*, *C*, *D*, and their inverses. They can be represented in two different notations with the values inside $\sum$ are as mid-terms to map. These are with input A,B,C,D:

$f(A, B, C, D) = \sum (5, 6, 7, 8, 9, 10, 11, 12)$

and

$f(A,B,C,D)=(\bar{A}BC\bar{D})+(A\bar{B}\bar{C}\bar{D})+(A\bar{B}\bar{C}D)+(A\bar{B}C\bar{D})+ (A\bar{B}CD)+(AB\bar{C}\bar{D})+$

Using the defined mid-terms, the truth table can be shown as:

#	*A*	*B*	*C*	*D*	*f(A,B,C,D)*
0	0	0	0	0	0
1	0	0	0	1	0
2	0	0	1	0	0
3	0	0	1	1	0
4	0	1	0	0	0
5	0	1	0	1	0
6	0	1	1	0	1
7	0	1	1	1	0
8	1	0	0	0	1
9	1	0	0	1	1
10	1	0	1	0	1
11	1	0	1	1	1
12	1	1	0	0	1
13	1	1	0	1	1
14	1	1	1	0	1
15	1	1	1	1	0

The input variables can be combined in 16 different ways. That's why the Karnaugh map has 16 positions and is arranged in a 4 × 4 grid.

The map is represented as:

CD \ AB	00	01	11	10
00	0	4	12	8
01	1	5	13	9
11	3	7	15	11
10	2	6	14	10

ABCD	ABCD
0000 - 0	1000 - 8
0001 - 1	1001 - 9
0010 - 2	1010 - 10
0011 - 3	1011 - 11
0100 - 4	1100 - 12
0101 - 5	1101 - 13
0110 - 6	1110 - 14
0111 - 7	1111 - 15

Kernel

This is the main component of computer systems. It is a bridge between applications and the actual data processing done at the hardware level. The responsibilities include managing the system's resources and the communication between hardware and software components. Kernel can provide the lowest-level abstraction layer for the resources especially processors and I/O devices that application software must control to perform its function. It typically makes these facilities available to application processes through inter-process communication mechanisms and system calls.

Different kernels are differently associated with different operating system depending on their design and implementation. Monolithic execute all the operating system codes in the same address space to increase the performance of the system. Micro run most of the operating system services in user space as servers, aiming to improve maintainability and modularity of the operating system. A range of possibilities exists between these two extremes.

Knapsack Problem

This is also known as Rucksack Problem. This has a set of items each with a weight and a value and determine the count of each item to include in a collection so that the total weight is less than or equal to a given limit and the total value is as large as possible. It derives its name from the problem faced by someone who is constrained by a fixed-size knapsack and must fill it with the most useful items.

The problem often arises in resource allocation with financial constraints, complexity theory, cryptography and applied mathematics etc. The decision problem form of the knapsack problem is the question— "can a value of at least *W* be achieved without exceeding the weight *M*?"

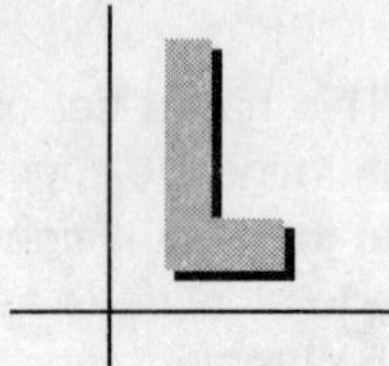

LAN

This stands for **L**ocal **A**rea **N**etwork**.** This is a network which interconnects computers and electronic communicating devices in a limited area such as a home, school, computer laboratory, or office building.

This is better than Wide Area Network for small area use due to higher data-transfer rates, smaller geographic area, and lack of a need for lines. Previously it was implemented with the help of token ring and connected wire but now this is using Wi-Fi. The use of Wi-Fi had enhanced its area due to portability.

Latch

This is also known as flip-flop**.** This is an electronic device having two stable states and can be used to store state information. The device can be used to change state by signals applied to one or more control inputs and will have one or two outputs. It is the basic storage element in sequential logic. This is the fundamental building block of digital electronics systems used in computers, communications, and many other types of systems.

There are several types of latch like J-K , D, T etc.

Latency

In the area of data communication it is similar to delay. This is an expression for how much time it will takes for a packet of data to go from one designated point to another. Latency is measured by sending a packet that is returned to the sender and the round-trip time is considered the latency. There are different methods to detect the latency.

LCD

This stands for **L**iquid **C**rystal **D**isplay. The earliest discovery leading to the development of LCD technology, the discovery of liquid crystals, dates from 1888. This is a flat electronic visual display or just video display that uses the light modulating characteristics of liquid crystals (LCs) to display the images.

They are used in a wide range of applications, including computer monitors, television, instrument panels, etc. It replaces the old display system like old colour monitor which uses cathode ray display. A latest technology LED had suppressed the LCD. LCDs are common in consumer devices such as video players, gaming devices, clocks, watches, calculators, and telephones. They are available in a wider range of screen sizes than CRT and plasma displays, and do not use phosphoruss, they cannot suffer image burn-in.

These are more energy efficient than CRTs. Its low electrical power consumption enables it to be used in battery-powered electronic equipments. It is an electronically modulated optical device made up of any number of segments filled with liquid crystals and arrayed in front of a light source or reflector to produce images in colour or monochrome. The most flexible ones use an array of small pixels.

Lexical Analyser

This is the part of Compiler. There are different layers of compiler and one of them is Lexical Analyser. The function of Lexical Analyser is known as Lexical analysis. It converts sequence of characters into a sequence of tokens. The specification of a programming language will often include a set of rules which defines the lexer. These rules usually consist of regular expressions and they define the set of possible character sequences that are used to form individual tokens or lexemes.

In programming languages delimiting blocks with tokens (e.g., "{" and "}") as opposed to off-side rule languages delimiting blocks with indentation, white space is also defined by a regular expression and influences the recognition of other tokens but does not itself contribute tokens. White space is said to be non-significant in such languages.

LED

This stands for **Light-Emitting Diode**. This is a light emitting source made up of semiconductor. This was introduced as a practical electronic component of red colour in 1962. But today it is available in different colours like ultraviolet and with very high brightness. This is used as lighting source due to low cost, longer lifetime, improved robustness, smaller size, faster switching and low consumption of electricity.

When a light-emitting diode is switched on, electrons are able to recombine with electron holes within the device and releasing energy in the form of photons. This effect is called electroluminescence and the colour of the light (corresponding to the energy of the photon) is determined by the energy gap of the semiconductor.

These are small in size less than 1 mm^2, and integrated optical components may be used to shape its radiation pattern. LEDs powerful enough for room lighting are relatively expensive and require more precise current and heat management than compact fluorescent lamp sources of comparable output.

Linear Grammar

A grammar is **linear** if it is context-free and all of its productions' right hand sides have at most one non-terminal. It follows linear language.

A linear grammar is G with $N = \{S\}$, $\sum = \{b, c\}$,

$S \rightarrow bSc$

$S \rightarrow \varepsilon$

Linked List

This is an algorithm used for storing and searching the data. This is a data structure consisting of a group of nodes which together represent a sequence. It stores data in node and each node is composed of a datum and a reference to the next node in the sequence. This structure allows for efficient insertion or removal of elements from any position in the sequence. An example is :

This is the simplest and most common data structures. They can be used to implement several other common abstract data structures, including stacks, queues, associative, and symbolic expressions.

The types of linked list are Double Linked List, Single Linked List, Circular Linked List. The principal benefit of a linked list over a conventional array is that the list elements can easily be inserted or removed without reallocation or reorganization of the entire structure because the data items need not be stored contiguously in memory or on disk. Linked lists allow insertion and removal of nodes at any point in the list and can do so with a constant number of operations if the link previous to the link being added or removed is maintained during list traversal.

LL Parsing

This is done through the Parser used in compiler design. This is a top-down parser for a subset of the context-free grammars. It parses the input from **L**eft to right, and constructs a **L**eftmost derivation of the sentence. The class of grammars which are parsable in this way is known as the LL grammars.

They takes tokens as input to parse. If such a parser exists for a certain grammar and it can parse sentences of this grammar without backtracking then it is called an LL(*k*) grammar where *k* is number of tokens. The LL parser is called an LL(*) parser if it is not restricted to a finite *k* tokens of look ahead, but can make parsing decisions by recognizing whether the following tokens belong to a regular language.

LL(1) grammars are general because the corresponding LL parsers only need to look at the next token to make their parsing decisions. Languages based on grammars with a high value of *k* have traditionally been considered to be difficult to parse.

Logic Gate

This is an electronics device implementing a function. It performs a logical operation on one or more logic inputs and produces a single logic output. Logic gates are primarily implemented using diodes or transistors acting as electronic switches. It could also be constructed using electromagnetic relays or relay logic, logic, pneumatic, optics, molecules, or even mechanical elements. With amplification, logic gates can be cascaded in the same way that Boolean functions can be composed. All of the algorithms and mathematics can be described with Boolean logic.

Low Level Language

This refers to either machine code or language. This is written as sequence of '0' and '1' by the compiler or interpreter in computer. But it may be obtained without the compiler and interpreter.

A program written in a low-level language can be made to run very fast, and with a very small memory footprint .An equivalent program in a high-level language will be more heavyweight. Low-level languages are simple but are considered difficult to use due to the numerous technical details which must be remembered.

LR Parsing

This is a parser which reads input from **L**eft to right and produces a **R**ightmost derivation. This is denoted as term LR(*k*) parser where the *k* refers to the number of unconsumed "look ahead" input symbols(token) that are used in making parsing decisions. The simplest LR parser could be made through putting value *k* is **1**.

It can handle a larger range of languages than parsing as well as better at error reporting, i.e., it detects syntactic errors when the input does not conform to the grammar as soon as possible. This is in contrast to LL(k) and LL(*) parser which may defer error detection to a different branch of the grammar due to backtracking which often making errors harder to localize across disjunctions with long common prefixes.

Depending on how the parsing table is generated, these parsers can be called simple LR parsers (SLR), look-ahead LR parsers (LALR), or canonical LR parsers. LALR parsers have more language recognition power than SLR parsers. Canonical LR parsers have more recognition power than LALR parsers.

LIFO

This stands for **L**ast **I**n **F**irst **O**ut. This is insertion and searching techniques in data structure. The queuing theory of data structure refers to the way items stored in some types of data structures are processed. By definition, in a LIFO structured linear list, elements can be added or taken off from only one end, called the "*top*". A LIFO structure can be illustrated with the example of a stack of trays. The last tray to be placed on top is also the first to be taken off the top.

Loader

This is the part of an operating system and responsible for loading programs. It is one of the essential stages in the process of starting a program, as it places programs into memory and prepares them for execution. Loading a program involves reading the contents of executable file, the file containing the program text, into memory, and then carrying out other required preparatory tasks to prepare the executable for running. Once loading is complete, the operating system starts the program by passing control to the loaded program code.

There are type of loader known as Bootstrap Loader which load all the programs at the ime of starting the computer. All operating systems that support program loading have loaders, apart from systems where code executes directly from ROM or in the case of highly specialized computer systems that only have a fixed set of specialised programs.

Log File

This is a file which keeps lists of actions that had occurred. This is essential in programming. This refers to either machine code or language. For example, Web servers maintain log files listing every request made to the server. With log file analysis tools, it's possible to get a good idea of where visitors are coming from, how often they return, and how they navigate through a site. Using cookies enables Webmasters to log even more detailed information about how individual users are accessing a site.

While doing programming software, developer put different Logger to trace the movement of executed code.

❑❑❑

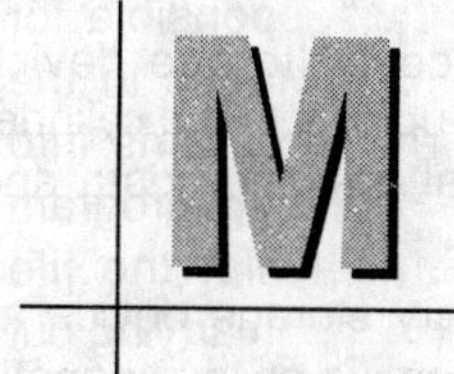

Machine Address

This is also known as the "host number" or "host address". This is the IP address that describe the details of any machine location and registration. The identifier of the network is known as "network number" while the identifier of the device is as "machine address". Security agencies catch the fraud entail activities through the Machine Address like— who sent any threatening mail, did unauthorised use of any banking credential etc.

Every machine has a unique Machine address.

Machine Language

This is binary code language readable to machine. This is also known as low level language. The set of instructions encoded as strings of binary bits are directly interpreted by a computer's central processing unit. There are machine languages based on different type of central processing unit. The machine language have unique interpretation including operations like arithmetical operations, incrementing a counter, saving data to memory, testing if data has a certain value, and so on. Compiler or Interpreters are used to convert high level language to low level language and low level language to high level language.

Magnetic Drum

This is a direct-access, or random-access storage device and also referred as drum. This is made-up of a metal cylinder coated with magnetic iron-oxide material on which data and programs can be stored.

Magnetic drums are used as a primary storage device as well as auxiliary storage device. The tracks on a magnetic drum are assigned to channels located around the circumference of the drum, forming adjacent circular bands that wind around the drum. A single drum can have up to 200 tracks and rotates at a speed of up to 3,000 rpm. The read/write heads deposit magnetized spots on the drum during the write operation and sense these spots during a read operation. This action is similar to that of a magnetic tape or disk drive.

Mainframe

This is an IBM powerful computer used primarily by corporate and governmental organizations for critical applications, bulk data processing such as census, industry and consumer statistics, enterprise resource planning, and financial transaction processing. This is also used as a operating system of computer. Several minicomputer operating systems and architectures arose in the 1970s and 1980s while large computer in 1970s.The minicomputer operating systems and architectures were known alternately as mini-mainframes or minicomputers like Digital Equipment Corporation's PDP-8 and the Data General Nova. Many defining characteristics of "mainframe" were established in the 1960s, but those characteristics continue to expand and evolve to the present day.

MIS

This stands for **Management Information System** and provides information needed to manage organizations efficiently and effectively. There are three primary resources involved — people, technology, and information. This is the backbone of modern big organisation. It helps in reducing the conventional way of keeping the records. It reduces the human effort in searching of informations as well as handling hard bound files. Management information systems are distinct from other information systems in that they are used to analyze operational activities in the organization. The term is commonly used to refer to the group of information management methods tied to the automation or support of human decision making, e.g., decision support systems, expert systems, and executive information systems.

Master-Slave Flip-Flop

This is the series of Flip Flop framed consecutively. Flip-Flop are used as to create storing devices. There are several types of Flip-Flop like J-k Flip-Flop, D Flip-Flop, T Flip-Flop etc. It is called master–slave because the second latch known as Slave in the series only changes in response to a change in the first known as master latch. The *pulse-triggered* Flip-Flop means that data is entered on the rising edge of the clock pulse but the output does not reflect the change until the falling edge of the clock pulse. By the help of D Flip-Flop the Master –Slave Flip-Flop can be pictorially represented as below:

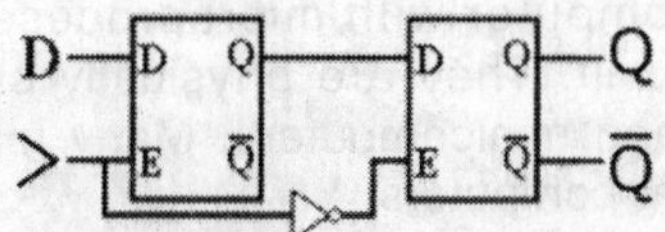

While its circuit diagram is as:

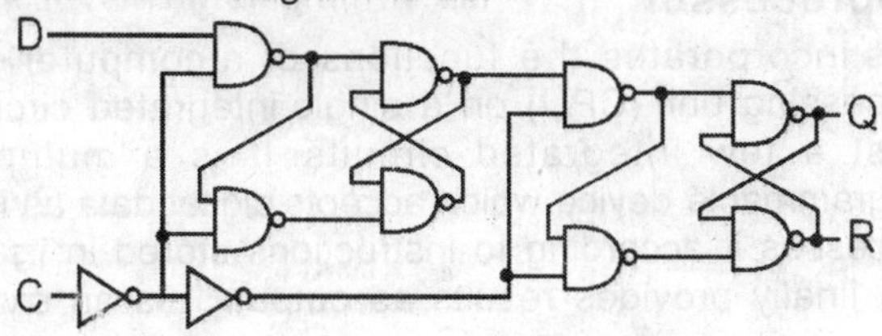

It is implemented with the help of two universal gate–NAND and NOT.

Memory Mapping

This is a technique which gives an application program the impression that it has contiguous working memory but in real practice it is physically fragmented and may even overflow on to disk storage.

Merger Exchange Sort

This is an algorithm of sorting to produce a single sequence of items ordered according to some rule from two or more previously ordered or unordered sequences. It do without changing the items in size, structure, or total number. Although more than one pass may be required for a complete sort, items are selected during each pass on the basis of the entire key.

Meta Assembler

The Assembler accepts a description of the assembly language to be recognized. Meta Assembler keeps information about the Assembler.

Microcomputer

This is a computer with microprocessor as its central processing unit. They are physically small compared to mainframe and minicomputers. Many microcomputers are also personal computers.

Microprocessor

This incorporates the functions of a computer's central processing unit (CPU) on a single integrated circuit or at most a few integrated circuits. It is a multipurpose, programmable device which accepts digital data as input and processes it according to instructions stored in its memory and finally provides results as output. It is an example of sequential digital logic, as it has internal memory. Microprocessors operate on numbers and symbols represented in the binary numeral system.

There are several types of microprocessors available in market like 8084, 8085, Celeron, AMD etc. Intel are the big cat in area of manufacturing microprocessor.

Mod-n Counter

This is a counter having N states. Its output frequency is f/N. For example a simple 4 bit binary counter is a mod 16 counter. Counter is an electronics device or software to count. Mod-n defines the number of input used in counter.

Modulation

This is the strengthening of electronic signal as an electronic or optical signal carrier. It can be applied to direct current mainly by turning it on and off, to alternating current and to optical signals. Modulators are used for modulation which are electronic devices. Morse code, invented for telegraphy and still used in amateur radio, uses a binary (two-state) digital code similar to the code used by modern computers. For most of radio and telecommunication today, the carrier is alternating current (AC) in a given range of frequencies.

Modulation happened over the amplitude, frequency, voltage, current etc.

Moore Machine

This is a finite-state machine whose output values are determined solely by its current state. This is part of Auto Mata theory.

MOSFET

This stands for Metal Oxide Semiconductor Field Effect Transistor. This is a transistor used for amplifying or switching electronic signals. Julius Edgar Lilienfeld has first discovered the basic principle of MOSFET in 1925. But first time the Bell Labs had given the name, Bipolar Junction Transistor, or simply Junction Transistor.

A voltage on the oxide-insulated gate electrode can induce a conducting channel between the two other contacts called source and drain in MOSFET. The channel can be of n-type or p-type, based on the n-channel it is called an nMOSFET and based on p-type it is called a pMOSFET. It is also known as pMOS and nMOS. It is by far the most common transistor in both digital and analog circuits, though the bipolar junction transistor was at one time much more common.

Mother Board

This is an electronic board used in computer CPU having all types of hardware like processor, RAM, Graphics card etc. This is also known as central printed circuit board. Many modern computers' motherboards holds many of the crucial components of the system, providing connectors for other peripherals. The motherboard is sometimes alternatively known as the main board, system board. In Apple computers it is known as the logic board.

Multiplexer

This is denoted as Mux. This is a device that selects several input signals as digital or analog signals and forwards the selected input into a single line output. It simplify the data communication by sending just one signal rather than sending different signals separately. A multiplexer of 2^n inputs has *n* select lines, which are used to select which input line to send to the output. Multiplexers are mainly used to increase the amount of data that can be sent over the network within a certain amount of time and bandwidth. This is also called a data selector.

An electronic multiplexer makes it possible for several signals to share one device or resource, for example, one A/D converter or one communication line, instead of having one device per input signal.

Mutual Exclusion

This is abbreviated to "mutex". This is an algorithms used in concurrent programming to avoid the simultaneous use of a common resource i.e., deadlock condition, such as a global variable, by pieces of computer code called critical sections. A critical section is a piece of code in which a process or thread accesses a common resource. The critical section by itself is not a mechanism or algorithm for mutual exclusion. A program, process, or thread can have the critical section in it without any mechanism or algorithm which implements mutual exclusion.

Examples of such resources are fine-grained flags, counters or queues, used to communicate between code that runs concurrently, such as an application and its interrupt handlers. The synchronization of access to those resources is an acute problem because a thread can be stopped or started at any time.

Masking

This is data that is used for bitwise operations. By using a masking multiple bits, byte, nibble, word etc. can be set either "on" or "off" or inverted from on to off or vice versa in a single bitwise operation.

MOS

This stands for Metal Oxide Semiconductor. Semicond-uctors are between conductors and Insulators. This is a metal insulator semiconductor structure in which the insulating layer is an oxide of the substrate material like silicon substrate. The insulating layer is silicon dioxide (SiO_2).

MICR Code

This stands for Magnetic Ink Character Recognition. This is a technology to processing cheques. All cheques have MICR code at the left hand corner. This is a unique 10 digit number.

Mail-bomb

This is a form of net abuse consisting of sending huge volumes of email to an address and an attempt to overflow the mailbox or overwhelm the server where the email address is hosted in a denial-of-service attack.

Modem

This is short form of Modulator-Demodulator. This is a device that modulates an analog carrier signal to digital information as well as demodulates such a carrier signal to decode the transmitted signal. The purpose behind this is to produce a signal that can be transmitted easily and decoded to reproduce the original digital data.

This is a device for availing internet facilities. It can be used over any means for transmitting analog signals from light emitting diodes to radio. The most familiar example of modem is a voice band modem that turns the digital data of a personal computer into modulated electrical signals in the voice frequency range of a telephone channel. These signals can be transmitted over telephone lines and demodulated by another modem at the receiver side to recover the digital data.

There are several such instruments to use as modem to avail internet facility like gazette.

MAN

This stands for Metropolitan Area Network. This is a computer network spread over a city or a large campus. It interconnects a number of local area networks (LANs) using a high-capacity backbone technology such as fiber-optical links. It provides up-link services to wide area networks and the Internet. It is different from the LAN which is used for small area coverage.

It can also depend on communications channels of moderate-to-high data rates. It might be owned and operated by a single organization but it usually will be used by many individuals and organizations. It might also be owned and operated as public utilities. They will often provide means for internetworking of local networks.

It supports LAN as well as WAN.

Manchester Code

This is also known as Phase Encoding, or PE. This is an encoding technique used in data communication by electronics means. This is a line code having encoding of each data bit has at least one transition and occupies the same time. It therefore has no DC component, and is self-clocking, which means that it may be inductively or capacitive coupled, and that a clock signal can be recovered from the encoded data.

Meta Language

This is a way of keeping information about language. It keeps statements about statements in another language. The expressions in a meta language are often distinguished from those in an object language by the use of italics, quotation marks, or writing on a separate line.

Middleware

This is computer applications software. This is used as middle man in designing software where user interacts with database. The software consists of a set of services that allows multiple processes running on one or more machines to interact. This technology evolved to provide for interoperability in support of the move to coherent distributed architectures. This often used to support and simplify complex distributed applications. It includes web servers, application servers, and similar tools that support application development and delivery. Middleware is especially integral to modern information technology based on XML, SOAP, Web services, and service-oriented architecture.

MIMD

This stands for Multiple Instruction Multiple Data. They operate several inputs as instructions simultaneously.

MIME

This stands for Multipurpose Intranet Mail Extension. This is used within a single organisation.

MPEG

This stands for Moving Picture Expert Group. This is way of storing video data. There are specific drivers to decode this format data and give the output as videos.

Multimedia

This is a media that uses a combination of different content forms. The term can be used as a medium with multiple content forms or as an adjective describing a medium as having multiple content forms. The term is used in contrast to media which use only rudimentary computer display such as text-only, or traditional forms of printed or hand-produced material. It includes a combination of text, audio, still images, animation, video, or interactivity content forms.

Multitasking

This is a way of doing several works simultaneously like listening music, doing with notepad etc. This is a method where multiple tasks known as processes share common processing resources such as a CPU.

In the case of old computing with a single CPU only one task is said to be *running* at any point of time. Multitasking solves the problem by scheduling which task may be the one running at any given time, and when another waiting task gets a turn. In reality only one process is execute at a time by the CPU but the interchange time between two processes is so less that it looks like multiple operations are going on. It is done with the help of dispatcher or switch techniques.

The act of reassigning a CPU from one task to another one is called a context switch. When context switches occur frequently enough the illusion of parallelism is achieved. Even on computers with more than one CPU called multiprocessor machines, multitasking allows many more tasks to be run than there are CPUs.

Multithreading

Multiprocessing are done with multithreading. But there are differences. Threads are small utility programmes. The threads have to share the resources of a single core, the computing units, the CPU caches and the translation look aside buffer (TLB).

Multithreading computers are distinguished from multiprocessing systems. Multiprocessing systems include multiple complete processing units while multithreading aims to increase utilization of a single core by using thread-level as well as instruction-level parallelism. As the two techniques are complementary, they are sometimes combined in systems with multiple multithreading CPUs and in CPUs with multiple multithreading cores.

❑❑❑

NAND Gate

This is one of the two basic universal logic gates from which any other logic gates can be fabricated. The other one is NOR logic gate. The AND gate can be represents as A . B, where A and B are two inputs. But when AND gate is linked with NOT gate then it is known as NAND gate. The function of NAND gate is reverse of AND gate.

The NAND gate are used to reverse the adding operation. The AND gate is represented as:

The pictorial view of NAND gate are:

Inputs		Outputs
A	***B***	***S***
0	0	0
1	0	0
0	1	0
1	1	1

Network Database

This is a database whicn runs in a network. It functions as client-server architecture in which database stores the information. Whenever any client requests the database regarding any information then database responds with appropriate answer like if data is present then deliver the data otherwise do excuse.

In real practice, the database in network lies scattered across different location throughout world.

Network Delay

This refers to delaying in transmission of data/packet/frame within the network. There are several reasons behind the delay in network like congestion, quality and quantity of electronic devices as well as software used.

Network Layer

This is layer 3 of the seven-layer OSI model of networking. The layer is responsible for packet forwarding including routing through intermediate routers. This is supported by other layers like adjacent layer to this which is the data link layer responsible for media access control, flow control and error checking. The network layer responds to service requests from the transport layer and issues service requests to the data link layer.

This provides the functional and procedural means of transferring variable length data sequences from a source to a destination host via one or more networks while maintaining the quality of service functions.

The different functions of the network layer are as:

- Maintaining the Connection: There are two types of connections for data communication –connection-less and connection-oriented; like IP is connectionless in which a frame/packet can travel from a sender to a recipient without the recipient having to send an acknowledgement. The Connection-oriented protocols exist at higher layers of that model.
- Maintaining Host addressing: A unique address of host is known as Host address. On the Internet, addresses are known as Internet Protocol (IP) addresses.
- Message forwarding:
  The networks are partitioned into sub-networks and connect to other networks for wide-area communications, The networks use specialized hosts, called gateways or routers to forward packets between networks. This is also of

interest to mobile applications, where a user may move from one location to another, and it must be arranged that his messages follow him. Version 4 of the Internet Protocol (IPv4) was not designed with this feature in mind, although mobility extensions exist. IPv6 has a better designed solution.

NMOS

This is a type of MOSFET. This stands for Non Metal Oxide Semiconductor.

Noise

This arises during data communication due to faulty technology and less efficient electronic instruments used. This is calculated in logarithmic form with signal processed.

Non-return-to-zero

This is known as NRZ code. This is a data communication techniques represented in binary code in which '1's are represented by one significant condition usually a positive voltage and '0's are represented by some other significant condition usually a negative voltage with no other neutral or rest condition. The pulses of this coding technique have more energy than a RZ (Return to Zero) code. Unlike RZ, NRZ does not have a rest state. This is not inherently a self-synchronizing code that is why some additional synchronization technique like a run length limited constraint, or a parallel synchronization signal must be used to avoid bit slip. The NRZ code requires only half the bandwidth required by the Manchester code for Data Signalling. The data flow in NRZ code is represented as :

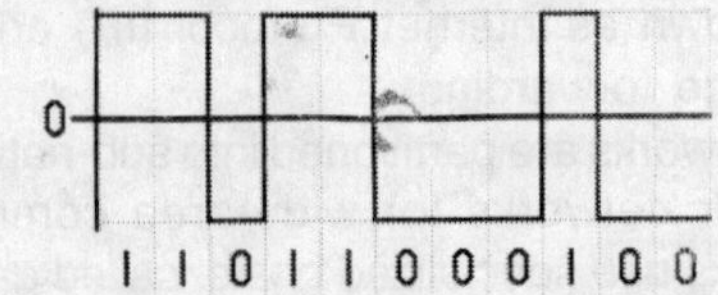

NOR Gate

This is a Universal digital logic gate. The functioning of NOR gate can be understood through truth table. The OR gate is written as A+B. Where A and B are input to the gate. OR is the result of the negation of the OR gate. The truth table are: The combinations of NOR gates can be combined to generate any other logical function. By contrast, the OR operator is *monotonic* as it can only change LOW to HIGH but not vice versa. The pictorial representation of NOR gate are:

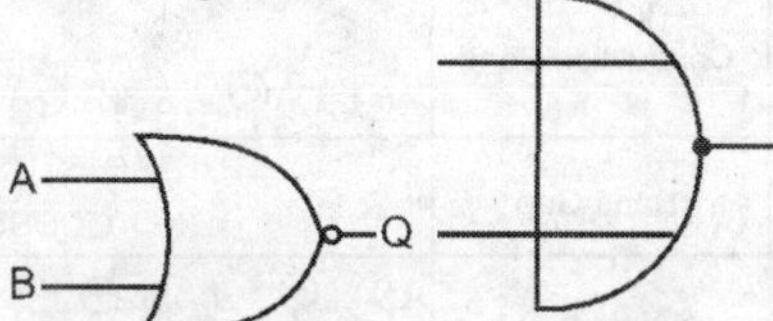

Inputs		Outputs
A	***B***	***S***
0	0	0
1	0	1
0	1	1
1	1	1

Normal Form

This is abbreviated as NF. This belongs to relational database theory provide criteria for determining a table's degree of vulnerability to logical inconsistencies and anomalies. The higher the normal form applicable to a table the lesser vulnerable it is to inconsistencies and anomalies. Each table has a normal form. A table always meets the requirements of its all normal forms.

There are generally three types of Normal Form- 1NF, 2NF and 3NF. From one towards 3 weightage of normal form change. First of all any table relation are in 1NF then in 2NF and then in 3NF. This is not an accurate description of how normalization typically works. A sensibly designed table is likely to be in 3NF on the first attempt furthermore, if it is 3NF, it is overwhelmingly likely to have of 5NF. Achieving the "higher" normal forms (above 3NF) does not usually require an extra expenditure of effort on the part of the designer, because 3NF tables usually need no modification to meet the requirements of these higher normal forms.

n-type Semiconductor

This is a type of extrinsic semiconductor where the dopant atoms are capable of providing extra conduction electrons to the host material like phosphorus, silicon etc. This creates an excess of negative i.e., n-type electron charge carriers. The view of n-type semiconductor with respect of temperature are:

	Conduction Band	c- c- e- c- e- c-
	Band Gap	
	Dopant Band	+ + + + + + +

Temperature = O Kelvin Temperature > O Kelvin

Null matrix

This is matrix having all elements zero.

n-p-n Transistor

This one of the two types of bipolar transistors consisting of a layer of P-doped semiconductor between two N-doped layers. The P layer of NPN is known as base. A small current entering the base is amplified to produce a large collector and emitter current.

Most of the NPN current is carried by electrons, moving from emitter to collector as minority carriers in the P-type base region. Most bipolar transistors use NPN because electron mobility is higher than hole mobility in semiconductors allowing greater currents and faster operation.

The diagram of NPN transistor is: 

Noise Ratio

This is represented as Signal-to-noise ratio which is often abbreviated as SNR or S/N. This is a measure that compares the level of a desired signal to the level of background noise. It is defined as the ratio of signal power to the noise power. A ratio higher than 1:1 indicates more signal than noise. While SNR is commonly quoted for electrical signals and can be applied to any form of signal.

Nano-computer

This is the logical name for a computer smaller than the microcomputer. It is also known as "mini" because it is a quite smaller than the original computers. More technically, it is a computer whose fundamental parts are no bigger than a few nanometers. For comparison, the smallest part of current state-of-the art microprocessors measures 45 nm.

Nibble

A nibble is a four-bit aggregation or half an octet. As a nibble contains 4 bits, there are sixteen (2^4) possible values, so a nibble corresponds to a single hexadecimal digit. The combination could be like:

0	0	0	0
0	0	0	1
0	0	1	0
0	1	0	0
1	0	0	0
0	0	1	1
0	1	1	0
1	1	0	0
0	1	1	1

No Parity

This refers to the lack of any error checking and the parity bit used for parity checking.

Null modem

This is a communication method to connect two DTEs (computer, terminal, printer etc.) directly using an RS-232 serial cable. The name stems from the historical use of the

RS-232 cable to connect two teleprinter devices to modems in order to communicate with one another. The communication was possible by instead using RS-232 to connect the teleprinters directly to one another.

The RS-232 standard is asymmetrical as to the definitions of the two ends of the communications link so it assumes that one end is a DTE and the other is a DCE e.g., a modem. With a null modem connection the transmit and receive lines are cross linked. Depending on the purpose, sometimes also one or more handshake lines are cross linked. Several wiring layouts are in use because the null modem connection is not covered by a standard.

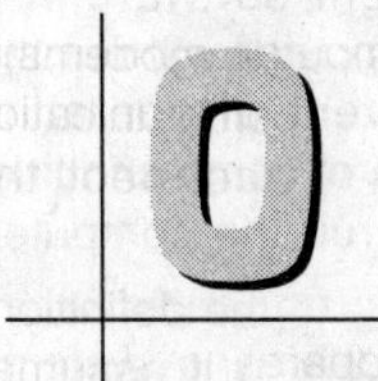

Object-Oriented Language

An OOP is a programming paradigm using concepts of "objects". Language like C++, Java, etc are known as object oriented language. It uses the methods including features such as data abstraction, encapsulation, messaging, modularity, polymorphism, and inheritance. Many modern programming languages now support OOP, at least as an option.

One's Complement

This is a system in which negative numbers are represented by the arithmetic negative of the value. An N-bit ones' complement numeral system can represent integers in the range $-(2^{N-1} - 1)$ to $2^{N-1} - 1$.

The ones' complement of a binary number is defined as the value obtained by inverting all the bits in the binary representation of the number i.e., swapping 0's to 1's and vice-versa. The ones' complement of the number behaves like the negative of the original number in most arithmetic operations. However, unlike two's complement, these numbers could not have widespread use because of issues like negative zero, end-around borrow, etc.

Operating System

This is a set of programs which manage computer hardware resources and provide common services for application software. This is the main part of system software in a computer system. It is difficult to run a computer without the use of operating system. Before the invent of operating system, computers were operated with help of command line. There always was a need of an expert to run the computer. But today even a child can operate it.

There are different techniques used in operating systems to regulate the process like scheduling, paging etc. Time-sharing operating systems schedule tasks for efficient use of the system and may also include accounting for cost allocation of processor time, mass storage, printing, and other resources.

For hardware functions such as input and output and memory allocation, the operating system acts as an intermediary between application programs and the computer hardware although the application code is usually executed directly by the hardware and will frequently call the OS or be interrupted by it. Operating systems are found on almost any device that contains a computer—from cellular phones and video game consoles to supercomputers and web servers.

The popular modern operating systems include Android, iOS, Linux, Mac OS X, XP, 98, Vista, Window 7 etc.

Optical Disc

This is a flat disc usually circular in shape made up of magnetic material used for storing the data. They come in different sizes and capacities of storing the data. There are two types of optical disk one is readable only and other is rewritable. The data is stored on the disc with a laser or stamping machine and can be accessed when the data path is illuminated with a laser diode in an optical disc drive which spins the disc at speeds of about 200 to 4000 RPM or more, depending on the drive type, disc format, and the distance of the read head from the centre of the disc.

There are different encoding techniques to encode the data which are stored in optical disc. The encoding material sits atop a thicker substrate usually polycarbonate which makes up the bulk of the disc and forms a dust defocusing layer. The encoding pattern follows a continuous, spiral path covering the entire disc surface and extending from the innermost track to the outermost track.

The data stored in optical disc are more reliable than other magnetic storing device like floppy and hard disc.

Oracle Database

This is commonly known as *Oracle RDBMS* or simply *Oracle.* This is an object-relational database management system produced and marketed by Oracle Corporation.

Larry Ellison, Bob Miner and Ed Oates developed the original version of the Oracle software. The name *Oracle* comes from the code-name of a CIA-funded project. Those similar to SQL language are used to access the database.

Ordered Tree

This is a tree where the children of each node have a designated order and can be referred to specifically. This is an algorithm of storing the data.

OR Gate

This is a digital logic gate which implements disjunction. It is represented as:

$A + B$, where A an B are two inputs of the gate.

The truth table of OR gate is :

A HIGH output (1) results if one or both the inputs to the gate are HIGH (1). If neither input is HIGH, a LOW output (0) results.

Inputs		Outputs
A	*B*	*A + B*
0	0	0
0	1	1
1	0	1
1	1	1

The OR gate is viewed as:

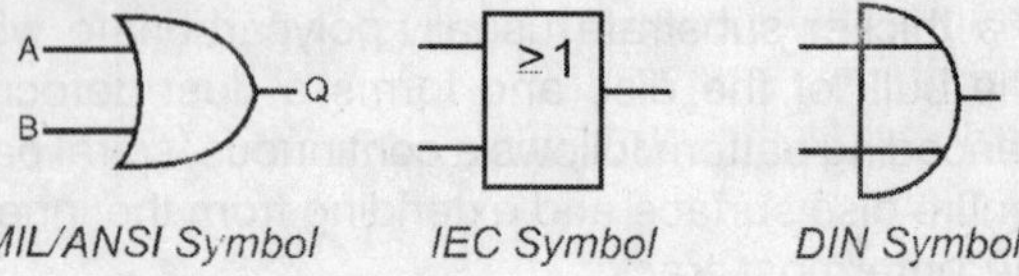

Overlay

This a technique to reduce the amount of memory used by a program.

Octal System

This is the base-8 number system that uses the digits 0 to 7 for encoding the data. Numerals can be made from binary numerals by grouping consecutive binary digits into groups of three beginning from the right. For example, the binary representation for decimal 72 is 1001000, which can be grouped into 001 001 000 — so the octal representation is 110.

In decimal systems each decimal place is a base of 10. For example: **7X10+2X1**

In octal numerals each place is a power with base 8. For example: **1X8X8+1X8+0X1**

Overloading

This is technique is used in programming language like C++, Java etc. It means having more than one method with the same name but a different list of arguments in the same class or in a combination of base and derived classes. They perform different functions based on their inputs.

ODBC

This stands for **O**pen **D**ata **B**ase **C**onnectivity. This is method to connect with databse. This is a standard C programming language interface for accessing database management systems. It makes independent of database systems from operating systems used while accessing the database. An application can use ODBC to query data from a DBMS regardless of the operating system or DBMS it uses. Like Java platform uses JDBC to link with ODBC to access the database. It is known as JDBC—ODBC driver.

It makes DBMS independence by using an *ODBC driver* as a translation layer between the application and the DBMS. The application uses ODBC functions through an *ODBC driver manager* with which it is linked, and the driver passes the query to the DBMS.

OMR

This stands for Optical Mark Recognition in the process of capturing human-marked data from document forms such as surveys and tests.

OODBMS

This stands for **O**bject-**O**riented **D**ata **B**ase **M**anagement System. This keeps information represented in the form of objects as used in object-oriented programming. When database capabilities are combined with object-oriented programming language capabilities the result became object-oriented database management system This is different from relational databases and belongs together to the broader database management system.

This allows object-oriented programmers to develop the product, store them as objects, and replicate or modify existing objects to make new objects. Because the database is integrated with the programming language, the programmer can maintain consistency within one environment. Relational DBMS projects maintain a clearer division between the database model and the application.

❑ ❑ ❑

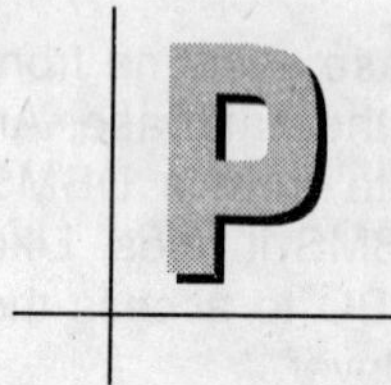

Package

This is a software suite or collection of related application or utility software. Whenever any programmers want to use the functionality of any software then they had to import the respective software from the package.

Packet

This is the unit of data which is routed between an origin and a destination on the Internet or any other packet-switched network. There are two methods of sending the data in data communication. One is through the packet and other is through the frame. When any file, e-mail message, HTML file, Graphics Interchange Format file, Uniform Resource Locator request, etc. is sent from one place to another on the Internet the Transmission Control Protocol (TCP) layer the TCP/IP used.

Packet Switching

This is a way of controlling the data communication traffic. The digital networking communications method groups all transmitted data – regardless of content, type, or structure into suitably sized blocks known as packets.

This is a delivery of variable-bit-rate data streams over a shared network. The traversing network uses the electronics equipment like adapters, switches, routers and other nodes. The packets are buffered and queued resulting in variable delay and throughput depending on the traffic load in the network.

This switching methods contrast with circuit switching which is a method sets up a limited number of dedicated connections of constant bit rate and constant delay between nodes for exclusive use during the communication session.

Paging

This is part of systems. This is a memory-management algorithm by which a computer can store and retrieve data from secondary storage for use in main memory. Whenever any process finds the page in main memory then it is known as page hit otherwise page fault. The pages are data from secondary storage in same-size blocks. Paging is an important part of virtual memory implementation in most contemporary general-purpose operating systems allowing them to use disk storage for data that does not fit into physical random-access memory (RAM).

The advantage of paging over memory segmentation is that it allows the physical address space of a process to be non-contiguous. Before the time paging was used, systems had to fit whole programs into storage contiguously which caused various storage and fragmentation problems.

Parallel Processing

The ability to carry out multiple operations or tasks simultaneously. The term is used in the contexts of both human cognition and parallel computing by machines. It makes programs run faster because there are more engines such as CPUs running it.

Generally computers have just one CPU but some models have multi-core processor chips. There are even computers with thousands of CPUs. Single CPU or single core computers perform parallel processing by connecting the computers in a network.

In real practice, it is difficult to divide a program that separate CPUs or cores can execute different portions without interfering with each other. However, this type of parallel processing requires very sophisticated software called distributed processing software.

Parallel Processing saves execution time because several CPUs do their work simultaneously rather than waiting for the output from the other CPU.

Parity Bit

This is a error detecting code. This is a bit which is added to ensure that the number of bits with the value one in a set of bits is even or odd. There are two types of parity bits: even parity bit and odd parity bit. It depends on requirement they are used.

Parity Check

This refers to the use of parity bits to check whether data has been transmitted accurately or not during data communication. This is added to every data unit normally as seven or eight bits which are transmitted. The parity bit for each unit is set so that all bytes have either an odd number or an even number of set bits. The most common form of parity checking is Even Parity.

For example– When two devices are communicating with even parity. The transmitting device sends data, it counts the number of set bits in each group of seven bits. If the number of set bits is even, it sets the parity bit to 0; if the number of set bits is odd, it sets the parity bit to 1. In this fashion, every byte has an even number of set bits. On the receiving side, the device checks each byte to make sure that it has an even number of set bits. If it finds an odd number of set bits, the receiver knows there was an error during transmission.

Parse Tree

This is also known as Concrete Syntax Tree or Parsing Tree. This is an ordered rooted tree which represents the syntactic structure of a string according to some formal grammar. The interior nodes are labeled by non-terminals of the grammar while the leaf nodes are labeled by terminals of the grammar while representing the Parse Tree.

The Parse trees may be generated for sentences in natural languages as well as during processing of computer languages such as programming languages. These are distinct from abstract syntax trees in which their structure and elements more concretely reflect the syntax of the input language.The example of Parse Tree is:

For– John hit the ball

```
              S
           /     \
         NP       VP
         |       /   \
       John     V     NP
                |    /  \
               hit  Det   N
                     |    |
                    the  ball
```

Parsing

This is the characteristic of Compiler. This is also known as syntactic analysis which process the analyzing of a text and made of a sequence of tokens to determine its grammatical structure with respect to a given formal grammar. Parsing can also be used as a linguistic term for instance when discussing how phrases are divided up in garden path sentences.

Parsing is also an earlier term for the diagramming of sentences of natural languages, and is still used for the diagramming of inflected languages, such as the Romance languages or Latin.

PASCAL

This is an imperative and procedural programming language designed in 1968 or 1969. This was published in 1970 by Nicklaus as a small and efficient language intended to encourage good programming practices using structured programming and structuring. A derivative known as Object Pascal designed for object-oriented programming was developed in 1985.

PCM

This is representation of Pulse-code modulation. This is a method used to digitally represent sampled analog signals in which the magnitude of the analogue signal is sampled regularly at uniform intervals. Each sample being quantized to the nearest value within a range of digital steps. This is the standard form for digital audio in computers and various others like Blue-ray, Compact Disc, DVD formats, digital telephone systems.

It has two basic properties that determine their fidelity to the original analog signal. One is the sampling rate which is the number of times per second that samples are taken and other is bit depth which determines the number of possible digital values that each sample can take.

PDA

This is known as Pushdown Automaton. This is a variation of finite automaton which makes use of a stack containing data. This differs from finite state machines in different ways like:

- They can use the top of the stack to decide which transition to take.

• They can manipulate the stack as part of performing a transition.

It chooses a transition by indexing a table from input signal, current state and the symbol at the top of the stack. This means that those three parameters completely determine the transition path that is chosen. Finite state machines just look at the input signal and the current state. Pushdown automata add the stack as a parameter for choice according to:

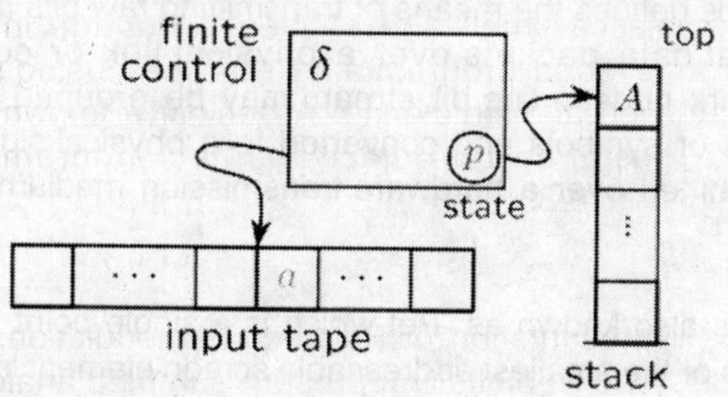

Phase Modulation

This is a modulation technique which represents information as variations in the instantaneous phase of a wave. The counterpart of this is Frequency Modulation.

This is not very widely used for radio transmissions because it requires more complex receiving hardware as well as there could be ambiguity problems in determining the signal. Example is the signal has changed phase by +180° or -180°.

But it is used however in digital music synthesizers such as the Yamaha DX7, even though these instruments are usually referred to as "FM" synthesizers.

Physical Layer

This is the first and lowest layer in the seven-layer OSI model of computer networking. It is a fundamental layer underlying the logical data structures of the higher level functions in a network. This is the most complex layer in the OSI architecture. The physical layer consists of the basic hardware transmission technologies of a network.

This provides an electrical, mechanical and procedural interface to the transmission medium. The shapes and properties of the electrical connectors, the frequencies to broadcast on, the modulation scheme to use and similar low-level parameters, are specified here.

This defines the means of transmitting raw bits rather than logical data packets over a physical link or connecting network nodes. The bit stream may be grouped into code words or symbols and converted to a physical signal that is transmitted over a hardware transmission medium.

Pixel

This is also known as **Pel** which is a single point in a raster image or the smallest addressable screen element in a device. This is the smallest unit of picture that can be represented or controlled over the screen.

Each pixel has its own address which corresponds to its coordinates. This is normally arranged in a two-dimensional grid which are often represented using dots or squares. More pixels typically provide more accurate representations of the originality. The intensity of each pixel is variable. In colour image systems, a colour is typically represented by three or four component intensities such as red, green, and blue, or cyan, magenta, yellow, and black.

Plasma Display

This is a type of flat panel display common to large TV displays 30 inches (76 cm) or larger. They are called "plasma" displays because the technology utilizes small cells containing electrically charged ionized gases or what are in essence chambers more commonly known as fluorescent lamps.

The quality of picture have huge difference between plasma television and normal cathode ray television.

PMOS

This stands for P-type metal-oxide-semiconductor. This uses p-type metal-oxide-semiconductor to implement logic gates and other digital circuits. Transistors of PMOS have four modes of operation: cut-off or sub threshold, triode, saturation and velocity saturation.

p-n Junction

This is formed by adding a P-type and N-type semiconductor created in a single crystal of semiconductor by doping the materials. It could be done by ion implantation, diffusion of doping, or by growing a layer of crystal doped with one type of doping on top of a layer of crystal doped with another type of doping. If two separate pieces of material were used then this would introduce a grain boundary between the semiconductors that severely inhibits its utility by scattering the electrons and holes. This is seen as:

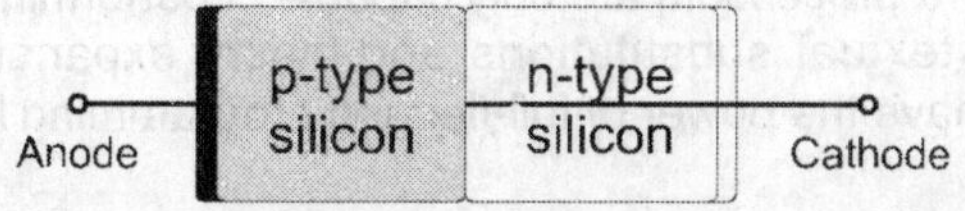

Port

This is either physical or virtual connection point of any electronic equipment. Physical network ports allow connecting cables to computers, routers, modems and other peripheral devices. Several different types of physical ports are available on computer network.

Postorder Traversal

This is a depth first traversal algorithm. It visits the root last while tree traversal. This is opposite to Preorder traversal which visits the root first. For Postorder traversal of a general tree one should follow:

- Traverse the left sub tree; and then
- traverse the right sub tree; and then
- visit the root.

Preorder Traversal

This is depth-first traversal algorithm. To do a preorder traversal of a general tree one should follow:

- Visit the root first; and then
- traverse the left sub tree; and then
- traverse the right sub tree.

Preprocessor

This is a program which processes its input data to produce output used as input to another program. It means it supports sequential processing. The output is known as pre-processed form of the input data which is often used by some subsequent programs like compilers. The amount and kind of processing done depends on the nature of the pre-processor. Some pre-processors are only capable of performing relatively simple textual substitutions and macro expansions while others have the power of full-fledged programming languages.

Presentation Layer

This is layer 6 of the seven-layer OSI model of networking. It serves as the data translator for the network. It is also called the syntax layer. It relieves the application layer of concern regarding syntactical differences in data representation within the end-user systems. An example of a presentation service would be the conversion of an EBCDIC-coded text computer file to an ASCII-coded file.

This is the lowest layer at which application programmers consider data structure and presentation instead of simply sending data in form of datagram or packets between hosts. This layer deals with issues of string representation — whether they use the Pascal method (an integer length field followed by the specified amount of bytes) or the C/C++ method (null-terminated strings, e.g., "rameshpublishing house\0"). The idea is that the application layer should be able to point at the data to be moved, and the presentation layer will deal with the rest.

Primary Memory

This is refers to physical memory which is internal to the computer. The word *main* is used to distinguish it from external mass storage devices such as drives, floppy, pen drive etc. The computer processor can manipulate only that data which is in main memory. Therefore, every program you execute and every file you access must be copied from a storage device into main memory or should be linked to it. The amount of main memory on a computer is crucial because it determines how many programs can be executed at one time and how much data can be readily available to a program. Random Access Memory is known as Primary Memory.

Program

A program is a specific set of ordered operations for a computer to perform, based on certain rules. Typically, the program is put into a storage area accessible to the computer. The computer gets one instruction and performs it and then gets the next instruction. The storage area or memory can also contain the data that the instruction operates on.

There are various programming techniques used to make programme like C, C++, Java, Cobol etc.

PROLOG

This is a general purpose logic programming language associated with artificial intelligence and computational linguistics. Its roots are in first-order logic or a formal logic. Unlike many other programming languages, Prolog is declarative i.e., the program logic is expressed in terms of relations, represented as facts and rules. A computation is initiated by running a *query* over these relations.

PROM

This stands for Programmable Read Only Memory. This is one-time programmable non-volatile memory. This is a form of digital memory where the setting of each bit is locked by a fuse or anti fuse. Such PROMs are used to store programs permanently. The key difference from a strict ROM is that the programming is applied after the device is constructed.

Protocol

This is a standard set of regulations and requirements that allow two electronic items to connect to and exchange information with one another. Protocols regulate data transmission among devices as well as within a network of linked devices through both error control and specifying which data compression method to use. Generally protocols decide the method of error checking, how to compact data (if required), how the transmitting device signals that it has concluded sending data, and how the receiving device signals that it has completed receiving data.

The most common Internet protocols are FTP (File Transfer Protocol), HTTP (Hypertext Transfer Protocol), TCP/IP (Transfer Control Protocol/Internet Protocol), and SMTP (Simple Mail Transfer Protocol).

Pseudo Code

The purpose of using pseudo code is that it is easier for persons to understand than conventional programming language code, and that it is an efficient and environment-independent description of the key principles of an algorithm.

There exists no standard for pseudo code syntax because as a program pseudo code is not an executable program. It resembles but should not be confused with skeleton programs including dummy code which can be compiled without errors. Flowcharts and UML charts can be thought of as a graphical alternative to pseudo code.

This is a compact and informal high-level description of the operating principle of a computer program or other algorithm. It uses the structural conventions of a programming language but is intended for human reading rather than machine reading.

Pseudo code typically omits details that are not essential for human understanding of the algorithm, such as variable declarations, system-specific code and some subroutines. The programming language is augmented with natural language descriptions details, where convenient, or with compact mathematical notation.

p-type Semiconductor

This is obtained by carrying out a process of doping i.e., adding a certain type of atoms to the semiconductor in order to increase the number of free charge carriers. When the doping material is added, it takes away weakly bound outer electrons from the semiconductor atoms. This type of doping agent is also known as an *acceptor material* and the vacancy left behind by the electron is known as a *hole*.

Pulse Train

This is also known as Pulse Wave. The pulse wave is also known as the rectangular wave, the periodic version of the function. This is a kind of non-sinusoidal waveform that is similar to a square wave but does not have the symmetrical shape associated with a perfect square wave. The exact shape of the wave is determined by the duty cycle of the oscillator. In many synthesizers, the duty cycle can be modulated sometimes called pulse-width modulation for a more dynamic timbre.

The graphic presentation of Pulse train are:

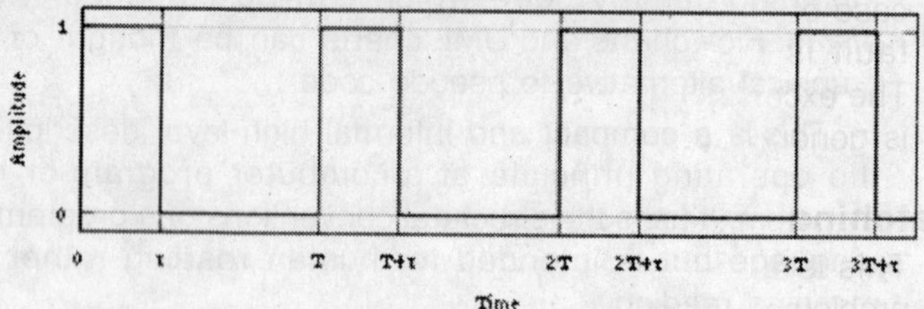

Punch Card

This is also known as punched card, IBM card, or Hollerith card. This is a piece of plastic card which contains digital information represented by the presence or absence of holes in predefined positions. The punched cards were widely used throughout the 19th century for controlling textile looms and in the late 19th and early 20th century for operating fairground organs and related instruments. They were used through the 20th century in unit record machines for input, processing and data storage. Early computers used punched cards, often prepared using keypunch machines, as the primary medium for input of both computer programs and data. Some voting machines use punched cards.

Today Punch Card is used as different purposes in big organisations; like giving access to employee.

Page Fault

This is a paging technique used by operating system for memory management. Whenever processor searches a page in main memory and does not find it, then it is known as page fault. This is a trap to the software raised by the hardware when a program accesses a page that is mapped in the virtual address space but not loaded in physical memory. In the typical case, the operating system tries to handle the page fault by making the required page accessible at a location in physical memory or kills the program in the case of an illegal access. The hardware that detects a page fault is the memory management unit in a processor. The exception handling software that handles the page fault is generally part of the operating system.

Patching

This is a piece of software designed to fix a particular problems, update a computer program or its supporting data. This includes fixing security vulnerabilities and other bugs, and improving the usability or performance. Though meant to fix problems, poorly designed patches can sometimes introduce new problems.

p-n-p Transistor

This is a junction transistor having an n-type semiconductor between a p-type semiconductor which serves as an emitter and a p-type semiconductor that serves as a collector. We can say, it is the combination of p-n transistor and n-p transistor in series.

Pointer

This is used in programming language like C, whose value refers directly to another value stored elsewhere in the computer memory using its address. For high-level programming languages, pointers effectively take the place of general purpose registers in low-level languages such as assembly language or machine code but may be in available memory. It references a location in memory and obtaining the value at the location.

Several languages support some type of pointer, although some have more restrictions on their use than others. As an analogy, a page number in a book could be considered a pointer to the corresponding page; dereferencing such a pointer would be done by flipping to the page with the given page number.

Process

This is an instance of a computer program which is being executed. It contains the program code and its current activity. Depending on the operating system, a process may be made up of multiple threads of execution which execute instructions concurrently.

Depends upon the weight of process, the execution time of machine is calculated.

PAN

This stands for Personal Area Network. This is a computer network used for communication among electronics devices including telephones and personal digital assistants. This can be used for communication among the personal devices themselves or for connecting to a higher level network and the Internet.

The implementation of PAN is occurred like Wireless PAN and wired PAN. A wireless personal area network is a PAN carried over wireless network technologies such as IrDA, Bluetooth, Wireless USB, Z-Wave, Zig Bee, or even Body Area Network. The reach of a WPAN varies from a few centimetres to a few meters. While the wired PAN uses physical devices to connect like computer buses such as USB and FireWire.

PDF

This stands for Portable Document Format. This is created by Adobe. This is used for read only in normal circumstances.

Peer-to-Peer

This is understood as communicating with same level. This is a distributed application architecture which partitions tasks or workloads among peers. Peers are equally privileged, equipotent participants in the application. They are said to form a peer-to-peer network of nodes.

Peers make a portion of their resources such as processing power, disk storage or network bandwidth, directly available to other network participants without the need for central coordination by servers or stable hosts. Peers are both suppliers and consumers of resources.

Like interaction between different layer of OSI model is known as Peer to Peer communication.

Pentium Processor

Pentium is the brand of Intel Coropration. The brand used for a series of x86-compatible microprocessors produced by Intel. In its most current form, a Pentium processor is a consumer-level product with a two-star rating, above the low-end Atom and Celeron products but below the faster Core i3, i5 and i7 lines as well as the high-end Xeon processors.

Photodiode

This is a type of photo detector capable of converting light into either current or voltage depending upon the mode of operation. The traditional solar cell used to generate electric solar power is a large area photodiode.

This is similar to regular semiconductor diodes except they may be either exposed to detect vacuum UV or X-rays or packaged with a window or optical fiber connection to allow light to reach the sensitive part of the device. Many diodes designed for use specifically as a photodiode use a PIN junction rather than a p-n junction, to increase the speed of response. A photodiode is designed to operate in reverse bias.

Plotter

This is a printing device for printing vector graphics. Plotters were widely used in applications such as design. They have generally been replaced with wide-format conventional printers. It is now common place to refer to such wide-format printers as "plotters," even though they technically aren't.

Polymorphism

This is a way of programming techniques used in language like C++, Java etc.

Private Network

The is a network that uses private IP address space in computer network. This follows the standards set by RFC 1918 and RFC 4193. These addresses are commonly used for home, office, and enterprise local area networks. Private IP address spaces were originally defined in an effort to delay IPv4 address exhaustion, but they are also a feature of the next generation Internet Protocol, IPv6.

Public Domain Software

This is software which has been placed in the domain. In other words there is absolutely no ownership such as copyright of the intellectual property that the software represents.

Public Key

This is a value provided by some designated authority as an encryption key that combines with a private key derived from the public key. It can be used to effectively encrypt messages and digital signature.

Private Key

This is an encryption/decryption key known only to the party or parties that exchange confidential messages. In traditional confidential key cryptography, a key would be shared by the communicators so that each could encrypt and decrypt messages. The risk in this system is that if either party loses the key or it is stolen, the system is broken. A more recent alternative is to use a combination of public and private keys. In this system, a public key is used together with a private key.

❑❑❑

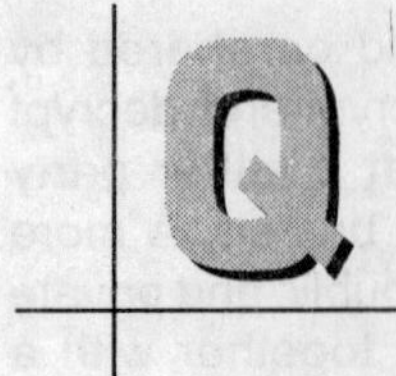

Query Language

This is a computer language used to make queries into databases and systems. Examples of query language are— SQL, Oracle etc. The commands are case sensitive.

Query languages can be classified according to database query languages and information retrieval query languages. The database query language attempts to give factual answers to factual questions while an information retrieval query language attempts to find documents containing information that is relevant to an area of inquiry.

Queue

This is an algorithm of abstract data type or collection in which the entities are kept in order. The principal operations on the collection are the addition of entities to the rear terminal position and removal of entities from the front terminal position. The queue functions as First-In-First-Out (FIFO) data structure i.e., the first element added to the queue will be the first one to be removed. This is equivalent to the requirement that once an element is added, all elements that were added before have to be removed before the new element can be invoked.

Types of queue are— Dqueue, Circular queue etc. A queue is an example of a linear data structure. The function of queue can be understood by the diagram:

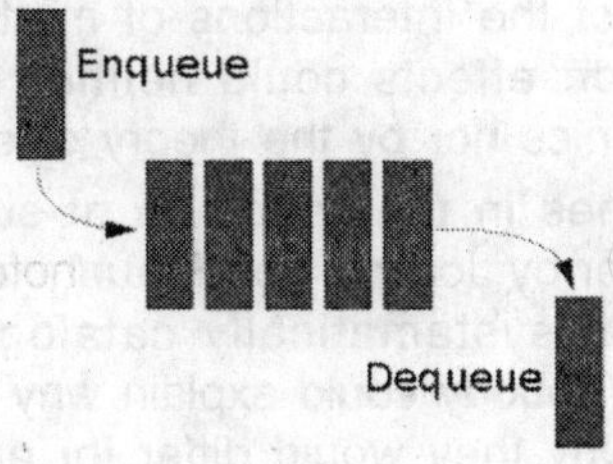

Quick Sort

This is a sorting algorithm developed by Hoare. The average complexity of this is $O(n\log n)$ while worst case is $O(n^2)$. Quick sort is often faster in practice than other algorithms.

Q-Band

This is the microwave part of the electromagnetic spectrum ranging between 33 to 50 GHz. Its above, and partly overlaps with K_a band ranging between 26.5 to 40 GHz. While sits below the V band ranging between 50–75 GHz in frequency.

The Q band is mainly used for satellite communications, terrestrial microwave communications and for radio astronomy studies such as the QUIET telescope. It is also used in automotive radar, and radar investigating the properties of the Earth's surface

Quantization

This is the procedure of constraining something from a relatively large or continuous set of values such as the real numbers to a relatively small discrete set such as—the integers.

Quantam Theory

This evolved as a new branch of theoretical physics during the first decades of the 20th century as an endeavour to understand the fundamental properties of matter. It began with the study of the interactions of matter and radiation. Certain radiation effects could neither be explained by classical mechanics nor by the theory of electromagnetism.

Particular lines in the spectrum of sunlight had been discovered earlier by Joseph Von Fraunhofer. These spectral lines were then systematically catalogued for various substances, yet nobody could explain why the spectral lines are there and why they would differ for each substance. It took about one hundred years, until a plausible explanation was supplied by quantum theory.

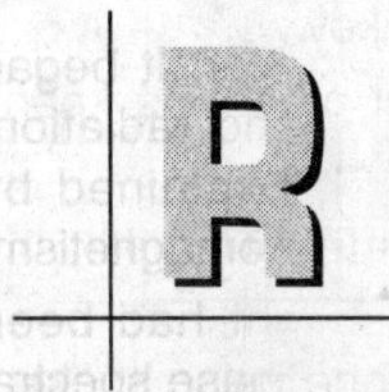

Race Condition

This can occur in electronic systems, especially logic circuits and in computer software, especially multithreaded or distributed programs. The term originates with the idea of two signals racing each other to influence the output first.

This is flaw in process by an electronics instrument whereby result of the process is unexpectedly and critically dependent on the sequence or timing of other events.

Radix Sort

This is a sorting algorithm. They sort data with integer keys by grouping keys by the individual digits which share the same significant position and value. But radix sort is not limited to integers because integers can represent strings of characters and specially formatted floating point numbers.

Each key of Radix Short first kept into one labelled buckets corresponding to the value of the rightmost digit. Each bucket preserves the original order of the keys as the keys are dropped into the bucket. There is a one-to-one correspondence between the number of buckets and the number of values that can be represented by a digit. The process repeats with the next neighbouring digit until there are no more digits to process. In brief:

- Take the least significant digit of each key.
- Group the keys based on that digit but otherwise keep the original order of keys.
- Repeat the grouping process with each more significant digit.

The sorting in second bullet is usually done using bucket sort or counting sort, which are efficient in this case since there are usually only a small number of digits.

RAM

This stands for Random access memory. This is temporary storage device and used as main memory in computer. Data resides in RAM till the power supply is persist. This comes in the form of integrated circuits which allow stored data to be accessed in any order. This comes in several form like SDRAM, DDRAM, Dynamic RAM. Read Only Memory (ROM) is used for permanently storing data as main memory.

The RAM is placed on motherboard of CPU in computer assembling. Generally it comes in multiple of 128 MB. The size of RAM decides the speed of any computer.

ROM

This stands for Read Only Memory. This belongs to storage medium used in computers and other electronic devices. This is one time writable device and data stored in ROM cannot be modified in normal circumstances. It is mainly used to distribute firmware which is very closely tied to specific hardware and does not need frequent updates like log table, input values etc.

Recursion

This is a method where the solution to a problem depends on solutions to previous instances of same problem. The output of previous solution becomes input for the next one and in this way final solution is achieved.

Most computer programming languages support recursion by allowing a function to call itself within the program text. Some functional programming languages do not define any looping constructs but rely solely on recursion to repeatedly call code. Computability theory has proven that these recursive-only languages are mathematically equivalent to the imperative languages, meaning—they can solve the same kinds of problems even without the typical control structures like "while" and "for".

Redundancy

It is the amount of wasted "space" during the transmission of certain data. This is equivalent to the number of bits used to transmit a message minus the number of bits of actual information in the message. Data compression is a way to reduce or eliminate unwanted redundancy while checksums are a way of adding desired redundancy for purpose of error detection while communicating over a noisy channel of limited capacity.

Reflexive Relation

This is a binary relation on a set for which every element is related to itself, i.e., a relation ~ on S where x~x holds true for every x in S. For example, ~ could be "is equal to".

Refresh

This is a technique to recharge a device with power or information. For example, *dynamic RAM* needs to be refreshed thousands of times per second otherwise it will lose the data stored in it. But modern RAM does not need to refresh.

Register

This is one of a small set of data holding places which are part of a computer processor. A register may hold a computer instruction, a storage address or any kind of data. Some instructions specify registers as part of the instruction. For example, an instruction may specify that the contents of two defined registers be added together and then placed in a specified register. A register must be large enough to hold an instruction – for example, in a 32-bit instruction computer, a register must be 32 bits in length.

Regular Expression

This is denoted as "regex" and "regexp". This is a part of compiler design. This provides a concise and flexible means for matching strings of text, such as particular characters, words, or patterns of characters. A regular expression is written in a formal language that can be interpreted by a regular expression processor which is a program that either serves as a parser generator or examines text and identifies parts that match the provided specification.

A regular expression is often called a pattern. The concept of regular expressions was first popularized by utilities provided by Unix distributions.

It is more concise to specify a set's members of expression by rules such as—a pattern than by a list. In most formalisms, if there exists at least one regex that matches a particular set then there exist an infinite number of such expressions. Most formalisms provide the following operations to construct regular expressions.

e.g., b|c*

(b|c)* denotes the set of all strings with no symbols other than *b* and c, including the empty string: {ε, *b*, c, cc, bc, cb, ...}

Regular Grammar

This is a formal grammar which describes a language. There are two types of Regular Grammar—Right Regular Grammar and Left Regular Grammar.

A **right regular grammar,** also known as right linear grammar is a formal grammar (N, Σ, P, S) such that all the production rules in P are of one of the following forms:

1. $A \to a$ — where A is a non-terminal in N and a is a terminal in Σ
2. $A \to aC$ — where A and C are in N and a is in Σ
3. $A \to \varepsilon$ — where A is in N and ε denotes the empty string, i.e. the string of length 0.

While in a **left reqular grammar,** also called left linear grammar, all rules obey the forms:

1. $B \to a$ — where B is a non-terminal in N and a is a terminal in Σ
2. $B \to Ca$ — where B and C are in N and a is in Σ
3. $B \to \varepsilon$ — where B is in N and ε is the empty string.

Relational Database

This is a database based on relational model theory. Differnt data and table used in storing data are liked to a certain relations. The software used in a relational database is called a relational database management system (RDBMS). This is the predominant choice in storing data over other models like the hierarchical database model or the model. The tables are represented as:

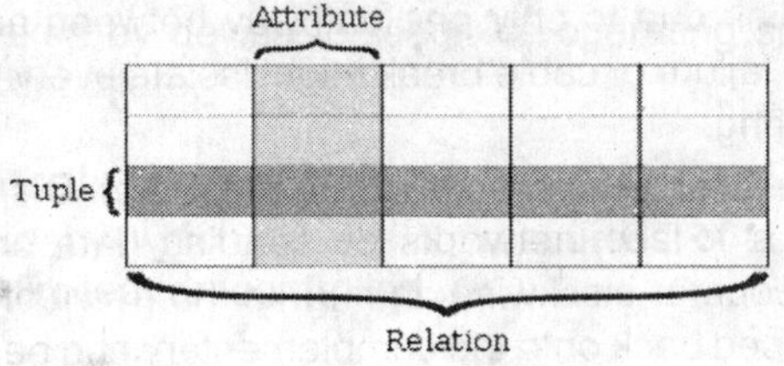

Remote Sensing

This is the way of wireless data communication through the satellite. In modern circumstances the term generally refers to the use of aerial sensor technologies to detect and classify objects on Earth by means of propagated signals.

There are two main types of remote sensing—Passive remote sensing and Active remote sensing. Passive sensors detect natural radiation which is emitted or reflected by the object or surrounding area being observed. Reflected sunlight is the most common source of radiation measured by passive sensors. Examples of passive remote sensors include film photography, infrared, charge-coupled devices, and radiometers. On the other hand, Active Remote Sensing emits energy in order to scan objects and areas where upon a sensor then detects and measures the radiation that is reflected or backscattered from the target. RADAR are examples of active remote sensing where the time delay between emission and return is measured, establishing the location, height, speed and direction of an object.

Ring Network

This is a network topology in which each node i.e., electronic instrument like computer is connects to exactly two other nodes forming a single continuous pathway for signals through each node. Data travels from node to node with each node along the way handles every packet.

The ring networks may be disrupted by the failure of a single link due to only one pathway between any two nodes. A node failure or cable break might isolate every node attached to the ring.

The problem is solved by the Fiber Distributed Data Interface (FDDI) networks by sending data on a clockwise and a counter-clockwise in ring. In the event of a break, data is wrapped back onto the complementary ring before it reaches the end of the cable, maintaining a path to every node along the resulting "C-Ring".

The connection of ring topology is viewed as:

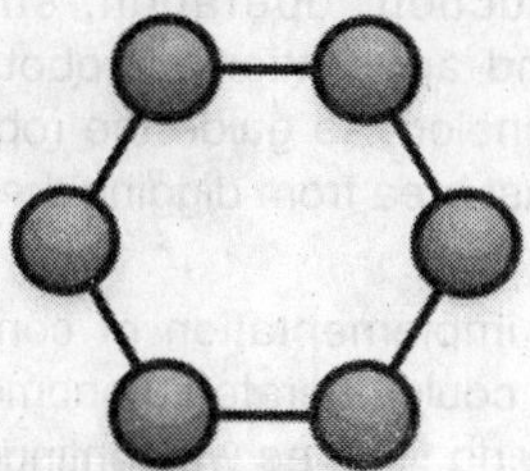

Ripple Counter

This is a single JK-type flip-flop with its J data input fed from its own inverted output. The circuit can store one bit and hence can count from zero to one before its overflow starts over from 0. This will increment once for every clock cycle and takes two clock cycles to overflow. For every cycle, it will alternate between a transition from 0 to 1 and a transition from 1 to 0. If this output is then used as the clock signal for a similarly arranged D flip-flop (remember to invert the output to the input), you will get another 1 bit counter that counts half as fast. Putting them together, yields a two-bit counter. This diagram of Ripple Counter is:

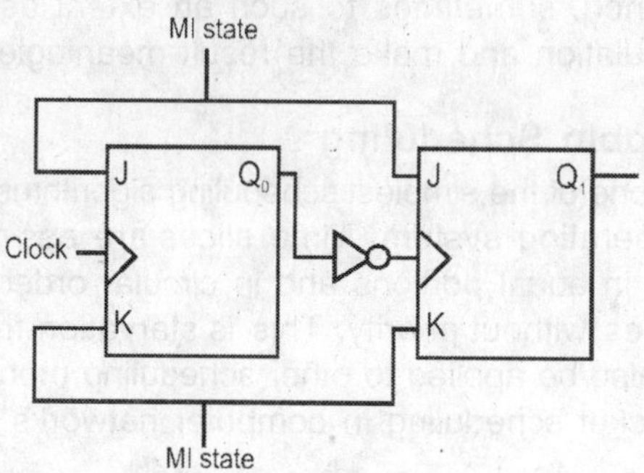

Robotics

This is related to the sciences of electronics, engineering, mechanics, mechatronics, and software and deals with the design, construction, operation, structural disposition, manufacture and application of robots. They use artificial intelligence technology to guide the robot. The application of robotics have vast area from digging the earth to doing human operation.

This is the implementation of concept and creation of machines which could operate autonomously . Today, robotics is a rapidly growing field, as we continue to research, design, and build new robots that serve various practical purposes, whether domestically, commercially, or militarily.

Round-off Error

This is also known as rounding error. This is a form of error. This is the difference between the calculated approximation of a number and its exact mathematical value. Numerical analysis specifically tries to estimate this error when using approximation equations and/or algorithms especially when using finitely many digits to represent real numbers. When a sequence of calculations subject to rounding error are made, errors may accumulate in certain cases known as ill-conditioned, sometimes to such an extent as to dominate the calculation and make the result meaningless.

Round Robin Scheduling

This is one of the simplest scheduling algorithms to processes in an operating system. Time slices are assigned to each process in equal portions and in circular order to handle all processes without priority. This is starvation-free algorithm. It can also be applied to other scheduling problems such as data packet scheduling in computer networks.

A round-robin scheduler generally employs time-sharing giving each job a time slot or *quantum* (its allowance of CPU time) and interrupting the job if it is not completed by then. The job is resumed next time a time slot is assigned to that process. In the absence of time-sharing or if the quanta were large relative to the sizes of the jobs, a process that produced large jobs would be favoured over other processes.

There exist several others type of scheduling like—Priority Scheduling.

Router

This is a computer networking device used for giving direction to the incoming signals. It is mandatory to control the traffic in data networking.

R-S Flip-Flop

This is Flip-Flop where one input is denoted as R and other is a S. This is similar to J-K Flip-Flop. The truth table of R-S Flip-Flop is:

R	S	Q	Q'	Comment
0	0	Q	Q'	Hold state
0	1	1	0	Set
1	0	0	1	Reset
1	1	?	?	Avoid

Based on the different inputs it shows performances like Hold, Set, Reset and Avoid. The circuit diagram of R-S Flip- Flop is:.

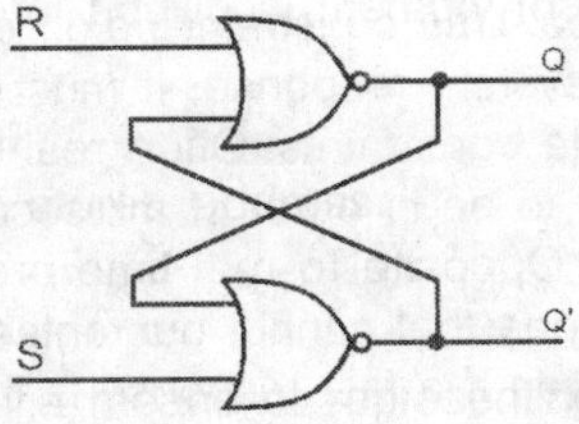

Runge-Kutta Methods

This belongs to family of implicit and explicit iterative methods for the approximation of solutions of ordinary differential equations. One member of the family of Runge–Kutta methods is so commonly used that it is often referred to as "RK4", "classical Runge-Kutta method" or simply as "*the* Runge–Kutta method".

An initial value problem be specified as follows:

$$y' = f(t, y), \quad y(t_0) = y_0$$

Radar

This is an object-detection system which uses radio waves to determine the range, altitude, direction, or speed of objects. It can be used to detect aircraft, ships, spacecraft, guided missiles, motor vehicles, weather formations, and terrain. The radar dish or antenna transmits pulses of radio waves or microwaves which bounce off any object in their path. The object returns a tiny part of the wave's energy to a dish or antenna which is usually located at the same site as the transmitter.

The shape, size and location define the capacity of radar. Generally, it is placed at high location to reduce the transmission cost as well as to improve its performance. The diameter of radar has significant parameters to define its strength.

Real Time Processing

This is the study of hardware and software systems which are subject to a "real-time constraint", e.g., operational deadlines from event to system response. It must guarantee response within strict time constraints. Often real-time response times are understood to be in order of milliseconds and sometimes microseconds. Opposite to real time processing a *non-real-time system* is one that cannot guarantee a response time in any situation even if a fast response is the usual result.

The real time processing is used in air traffic, internet ticketing of railway, IP TV etc. On the other hand Non-real time processing is used for mailing etc. There are minimum data speed requisite for real time processing.

Rectifier

The process of converting alternating current to direct current is known as rectification. The electrical device used in this is known as Rectifier. Physically, it takes a number of forms including vacuum tube diodes, mercury-arc valves, solid-state diodes, silicon-controlled rectifiers and other silicon-based semiconductor switches. Early radio receivers, called crystal radios, used a "cat's whisker" of fine wire pressing on a crystal of galena to serve as a point-contact rectifier or "crystal detector".

Reference Address

This is a value which enables a program to indirectly access a particular data item such as a variable or a record used in the computer's memory or in some other storage device. The reference is said to **refer** to the data item and accessing those data is called dereferencing the reference.

Reflected Code

This is also known as Gray code after the name of its inventor Gray. This is a binary numeral system where two successive values differ in only one bit. It is a non-weighted code.

Remote Computer

This is a computer to which a user does not have physical access but they can access or manipulate via some kind of network. Like a user seated in India can access a computer in USA.

Remote desktop software allows a person to control a computer from another computer. This allows the user to change anything on the linear computer, and access all of the file contents.

Reset

It means to clear any pending errors or events and bring a system to normal condition or initial state usually in a controlled manner in data communication. It is usually done in response to an error condition when it is impossible or undesirable for a processing activity to proceed and all error recovery mechanisms fail. A storage program would normally perform a "reset" if a command times out and error recovery schemes like retry or abort also fail.

There always exits a 'Reset' button in CPU of desktop computer.

RCTL

This stands for Resistor-Capacitor-Transistor Logic. This is a logical device made up through the resistor, capacitor and transistor.

RISC

This stands for Reduced Instruction Set Computing. This is a CPU design strategy based on the insight that simplified instructions can provide higher performance if this simplicity enables much faster execution of each instruction. This is opposite to CISC stands for Complex Instruction Set Computing.

❑ ❑ ❑

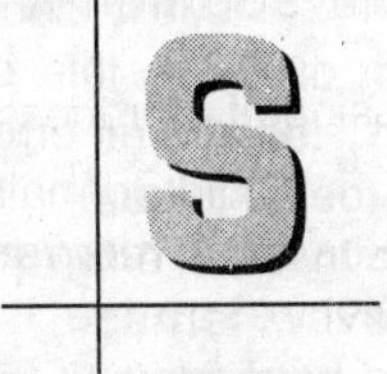

Sampling

This is concerned with the selection of a subset of data from a collection of data to estimate characteristics of the whole data. This is used in statistics and survey methodology.

The sampling method is used to avoid cost of too much high data.

There are three main advantages of sampling — the cost is lower, data collection is faster, and since the data set is smaller, it is possible to ensure homogeneity and to improve the accuracy and quality of the data.

Scanner

This is another name of lexical analyser for computer designing. In electronic term, it is an electronic device to scan the documents and pictures.

Scheduling

This is an algorithm by which threads, processes or data flows are given access to system resources like printer, scanner etc. This is used to avoid deadlock and starvation condition. The need for a scheduling algorithm arises from the requirement for most modern systems to perform multitasking.

The scheduler is concerned mainly with:

- Throughput – number of processes that complete their execution per time unit.

- Latency, specifically:
- Turnaround – total time between submission of a process and its completion.
- Response time – amount of time it takes from when a request was submitted until the first response is produced.
- Fairness / Waiting Time – Equal CPU time to each process (or more generally appropriate times according to each process' priority).

There are several types of scheduling algorithm used like Round Robin Scheduling, Priority Scheduling etc.

Schema

This is used as database system in which structure described in a formal language supported by the database management system. It refers to the organization of data to create a blueprint of how a database will be constructed, i.e., dividing into tables. Each table may be linked to the others.

The formal definition of database schema is a set of formulae that specify integrity constraints imposed on the database. All constraints are expressible in the same language. A database can be seen in terms of logic as a structure in a realization of the database language. The states of a created conceptual schema are transformed into an explicit mapping, the database schema. This describes how real world entities are modelled in the database.

Schottky TTL

Here TTL stands for Transistor- Transistor Logic. The Schottky diode is a semiconductor-metal diode having a low cut-in voltage typically 300 mili volts compared to 600 mV for other common semiconductor diodes. It also has a relatively high switching speed. This is relatively fast bipolar logic which is normally produced in integrated-circuit form.

In this the low cut-in voltage of the diode limits the base-collector voltage to about 400 mV, which prevents the transistor falling into saturation. This results in faster switching times for the transistors constructed in this way.

Secondry Memory

This is also known as external memory or auxiliary storage. Secondary storage is non volatile in nature as does not lose the data when the device is powered down. It comes in different forms like compact disk, hard disk etc.

This differs from primary storage and not directly accessible by the CPU. The CPU directly only accesses primary memory. The computer usually uses its input/output channels to access secondary storage and transfers the desired data using intermediate area in primary storage. Per unit, it is typically also two orders of magnitude less expensive than primary storage. Consequently, modern computer systems typically have two orders of magnitude more secondary storage than primary storage and data are kept for a longer time there.

Second Generation Computer

Transistors marked the start of the second generation computers. Transistors replaced the vacuum tubes used in the first generation computers.

In Second Generation computers, the instructions (program) could be stored inside the computer's memory. The second generation computers replaced Machine language with the assembly language. Even though complex in itself, Assembly language was much easier than the binary code.

Second generation computers started showing linking of utilities such as printers, disk storage and operating systems. High-level languages such as COBOL (Common Business-Oriented Language) and FORTRAN (Formula Translator) were used, and they are still used for some applications nowadays.

Self-Compiling Compiler

Many compilers for popular languages were first written in another language implementation and then rewrite their own source language. Overwrite provides a source for the compiler, which can then be compiled with a compiler written in the original implementation language.

Semantic Error

It is a logic error or bug in a program which causes it to operate incorrectly, but not to terminate abnormally (or crash). It produces unintended or undesired output or other behaviour. It may not be immediately recognized as such. It occur in both compiled and interpreted languages. Unlike a program with a syntax error, a program with a logic error is a valid program in the language, though it does not behave as intended.

Semaphore

This is a variable or abstract data type which provides a useful abstraction for controlling access by multiple processes to a common resource in a parallel programming environment. Semaphores are useful tools in the prevention of race conditions and deadlocks.

There are generally two types of semaphores—Counting semaphores and Binary semaphores. Semaphores which allow an arbitrary resource count are called counting semaphores while semaphores which are restricted to the values 0 and 1 (or locked/unlocked, unavailable/available) are called binary semaphores.

Semiconductor

This is a material having electrical conductivity between non-conductor and conductor. The electrical conductivity arises due to electron flow due to temperature. The electronic properties and the conductivity of a semiconductor can be changed in a controlled manner by adding very small quantities of other elements called "dopants", to the intrinsic material.

Silicon is used to create most semiconductors commercially. Other semiconductor materials are germanium, gallium arsenide, and silicon carbide.

A pure semiconductor is often called an "intrinsic" semiconductor. In crystalline silicon typically, this is achieved by adding impurities of boron or phosphorus to the melt and then allowing the melt to solidify into the crystal.

Serial Adder

This is a digital circuit to performs binary addition bit by bit. The serial full adder has three single-bit inputs for the numbers to be added and the carry in. There are two single-bit outputs for the sum and carry out. The carry-in signal is the previously calculated carry-out signal. The addition is performed by adding each bit, lowest to highest, one per clock cycle.

Server

This is a physical computer or a hardware system dedicated to running one or more services as a host, to serve the needs of users of the other computers on the network called client. In the context of Internet Protocol (IP) networking, a **server** is a program that operates as a socket listener.

The client-server architecture is most dominating structure in data communication. Thus, the "server" performs some computational task on behalf of "clients". The clients either run on the same computer or connect through the network.

There are several types of server—database server, file server, mail server, print server, web server, etc.

Session Layer

This is layer 5 of the seven-layer OSI model of networking. It provides the mechanism for opening, closing and managing a session between end-user application processes. Communication sessions consist of requests and responses that occur between applications.

These are commonly used in application environments which make use of remote procedure calls. An example of a session-layer protocol is the OSI protocol suite session-layer protocol, also known as X.235 or ISO 8327. In case of a connection loss, this protocol may try to recover the connection. If a connection is not used for a long period, the session-layer protocol may close it and re-open it. It provides for either full duplex or half-duplex operation and provides synchronization points in the stream of exchanged messages.

Seven Layer Reference Model

This is known as Open Systems Interconnection model (OSI model). This is Open Systems Interconnection effort at the International Organization for Standardization. This is a prescription of characterizing and standardizing the functions of a communication system in terms of abstraction layers. Similar communication functions are grouped into logical layers. An instance of a layer provides service to its upper layer instances while receiving service from the layer below. This is layered as:

OSI Model			
	Data unit	Layer	Function
Host layers	Data	7. Application	Network process to application
		6. Presentation	Data representation, encryption and decryption, convert machine dependent data to machine independent data
		5. Session	Interhost communication, managing sessions between applications
	Segments	4. Transport	End-to-end connections, reliability and flow control
Media layers	Packet/Datagram	3. Network	Path determination and logical addressing
	Frame	2. Data link	Physical addressing
	Bit	1. Physical	Media, signal and binary transmission

Shift Counter

This is a synchronous counter uses clocked flip-flops as a shift register. Data may be propagated from left to right or from right to left between the flip-flops.This is achieved by the application of a clock or count pulse. Counting is started by setting the contents of the shift register to logic 0 or 1. This also loading the leftmost or rightmost flip-flop with a logic 1 or logic 0.

The capacity of counter is identified by its bits handling capacity. An *m*-bit counter keeps *m* flip-flops and require *m* clock pulses to shift this 1 or 0 to the rightmost or leftmost flip-flop respectively. The position in the register of the 1 or 0 thus acts as a count of the number of pulses received since application of the load.

Shift Register

This is a cascade of flip-flops. The output of previous register becomes input of next register and so on. They share the same clock. In such circuit, shifts by one position the one-dimensional "bit array" stored in it shifting in the data present at its input and *shifting out* the last bit in the array when enabled to do so by a transition of the clock input.

Shift registers can have both characteristics parallel and serial inputs and outputs. This may be multidimensional such that its "data in" input and stage outputs are themselves bit arrays. This is implemented simply by running several shift registers of the same bit-length in parallel.

Shortest–path Algorithm

This is an algorithm of finding a path between two vertices or nodes in a graph. The algorithm keeps sum of the weights of its constituent edges during traversal minimized. This is used as finding the quickest way to get from one location to another on a road map. The path between two vertices or nodes is assigned some fixed weight. The algorithm calculated is sum of this weight while traversing. There are several algorithm used for implementing this. This could be understood by the graph:

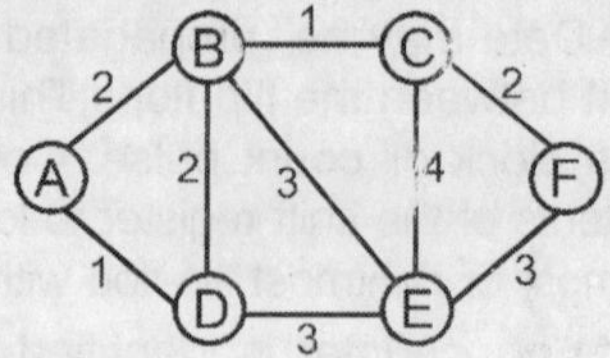

Sibling

They are same parents' child. It means if X and Y are children of parents A and B then X and Y are siblings. In upper graph B and D are linked to A. Here B and D are siblings A.

Signal-to-noise Ration

This is abbreviated SNR or S/N. This is a measure used to compare the level of a desired signal to the level of background noise. This is defined as the ratio of signal power to the noise power. A ratio higher than 1:1 indicates more signal than noise.

This can be applied to any form of signal but mainly used for electrical signals. Signal-to-noise ratio is defined as the power ratio between a signal and the background noise.

This is represented as: $SNR = \frac{P_{signal}}{P_{noise}}$.

Simplex Code Manager

Simplex was developed by a team of community planners who wanted to allow municipalities to more effectively share their land development code with the public and other users. This is an online tool which a municipality can use to create their own website to post their land development regulations and related documents online in a unique user-friendly format.

Single Threading

This is the processing of one command at a time and uses one thread only. Thread is a small computer software which handles different requests. The use of multithreading replaces the use of single threading. The multithreading enhances the capacity of computing and used to implement multitasking and multiprocessing which could not be possible by the single threading.

Single Linked List

The list is an algorithm used for inserting and searching the data in different data structure. This is two dimensional method to do this. This is a recursive data structure because it contains a pointer to a *smaller* object of the same type.

Each node have two components in singly linked list – one is data and other is pointer to keeps address of next data. But they do not keep address of previous data. Linear singly linked lists also allow tail-sharing, the use of a common final portion of sub-list as the terminal portion of two different lists. In particular, if a new node is added at the beginning of a list, the former list remains available as the tail of the new one — a simple example of a persistent data structure. This can be represented as:

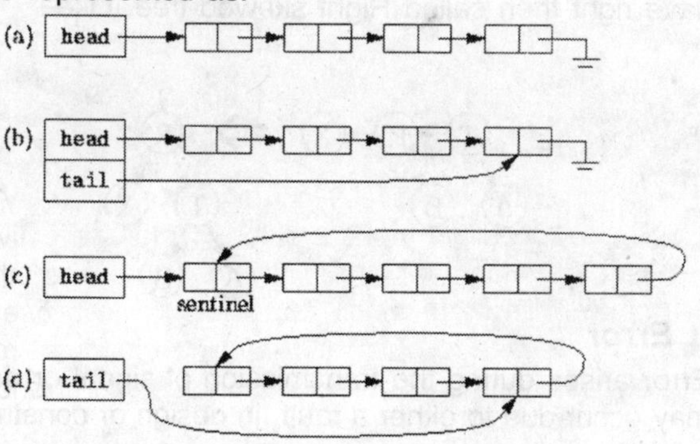

There are several other types of list algorithm available to eradicate the problems of single linked list–double linked list, circular linked list etc. While doubly linked and or circular lists have advantages over singly linked linear lists, linear lists offer some advantages that make them preferable in some situations.

Singular Matrix

This is a matrix which do not have inverse. Its determinants are equivalent to zero. For example:

$$\begin{bmatrix} 0 & 0 \\ 0 & 0 \end{bmatrix} \cdot \begin{bmatrix} 0 & 0 \\ 0 & 1 \end{bmatrix} \cdot \begin{bmatrix} 0 & 0 \\ 1 & 0 \end{bmatrix} \cdot \begin{bmatrix} 0 & 0 \\ 1 & 1 \end{bmatrix} \cdot \begin{bmatrix} 0 & 1 \\ 0 & 0 \end{bmatrix}$$

$$\begin{bmatrix} 0 & 1 \\ 0 & 1 \end{bmatrix} \cdot \begin{bmatrix} 1 & 0 \\ 0 & 0 \end{bmatrix} \cdot \begin{bmatrix} 1 & 0 \\ 1 & 0 \end{bmatrix} \cdot \begin{bmatrix} 1 & 1 \\ 0 & 0 \end{bmatrix} \cdot \begin{bmatrix} 1 & 1 \\ 1 & 1 \end{bmatrix}$$

Skewed Tree

This is a tree which is not balanced. It means right-hand side and left-hand side of the tree do not have equal number of children. Tree is the three dimensional data structure. If only tree had left sub tree then called Left skewed tree and if only have right then called Right skewed tree. Like–

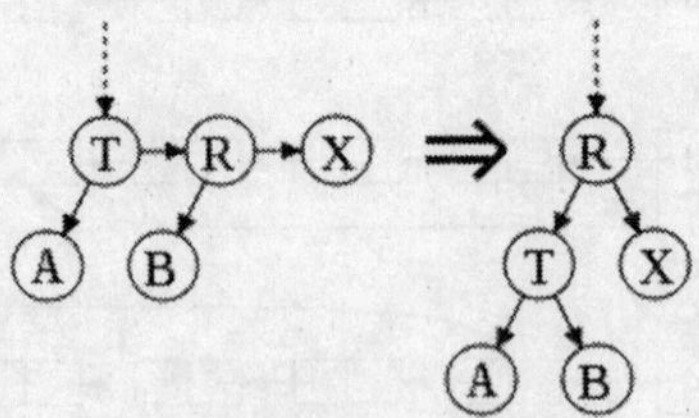

Soft Error

Error arises during the transmission of signal or datum. This may occur due to either a fault in design or construction or a faulty device. A soft error is also a signal or datum which is wrong, but is not assumed to imply such a mistake or breakage. After observing a soft error, there is no implication that the system is any less reliable than before.

Software

The software is a set of computer programs, procedures, and associated documentation concerned with the operation of a data processing system. This is a deck of computer programs and related data which provides the instructions for telling a computer what to do and how to do it.

Software performs the function of the program and implements either by directly providing instructions to the computer hardware or by serving as input to another piece of software. In contrast to hardware, software "cannot be touched". Sometimes the term includes data that has not traditionally been associated with computers, such as film, tapes, and records.

There are mainly two types of software— Application software and System software. System software are responsible to handle the hardware part of devices like hard disk, processor, CD-ROM etc. On the other hand, application software are associated with providing different types of services to users like listening music, notepad, WordPad etc.

There are different languages used to make a software like C, C++, Java, COBOL, PASCAL etc. Software are deployed as jar file on the server.

Software Engineering

This is the application of Engineering to software because it integrates significant mathematics, computer science and practices whose origins are in Engineering. This is the application of a systematic, disciplined, quantifiable approach to the development, operation, and maintenance of software. This also includes the study of these approaches that is the application of engineering to software.

The term software engineering first appeared in the 1968 at NATO Software Engineering Conference and was meant to provoke thought regarding the perceived "software crisis" at that time.

Software Life Cycle

This is the set of different phases of software product preparation from beginning to end. This includes—requirements gathering phase, analysis of data phase, design of software phase, development of software phase, testing of software phase or validation phase, installation phase, operation phase, maintenance phase, and retirement phase. Generally this is divided into 7 phases by adding several last phases into one phase.

The longest phase is designing phase. There are different techniques for software development like spiral, waterfall etc. The development process tends to run iteratively through these phases rather than linearly. Other processes associated with a software product are: quality assurance, marketing, sales and support.

Software Prototyping

This is the activity of creating prototypes of software applications. It is an activity that can occur in software development and is comparable to prototyping as known from other fields, such as mechanical engineering or manufacturing.

Software Quality Assurance

This is monitoring the software engineering processes and methods used to ensure quality of software delivered. There are several methods for assuring the quality of software like

ISO or a model such as CMMI. They certified software based on different level like CMMI 1, CMMI 2 to CMMI 5. Similarly, ISO 9000, ISO 9001 etc. This is organized into goals, commitments, abilities, activities, measurements, and verifications.

They encompass the entire software development process which includes processes such as requirements definition, software design, coding, source code control, code reviews, change management, configuration management, testing, release management, and product integration.

Sorting

This is an algorithm that puts elements in a certain order. There are several types of sorting algorithm present like—Merge sort, Heap sort, Radix sort etc. The characteristics of the sorting is calculated based on its complexity i.e., time taken to run the application.

Efficient sorting is important for optimizing the use of other algorithms such as search and merge algorithms which require sorted lists to work correctly.

Source Code

This is main text written using the format and syntax of the language. This is used by the other code. Such a language is specially designed to facilitate the work of computer programmers because it can be automatically translated to binary machine code which the computer can directly read and execute.

The interpreter are used to translate it to machine code and executes it on the fly. Most computer applications are distributed in a form that includes executable files, but not their source code. If the source code was included it would be useful to a user, programmer, or system administrator who may wish to modify the program or understand how it works. At the same time it may give rise to software piracy.

Spanning Tree

These are connected and undirected graphs composed of all the vertices and edges of graph. Informally, a spanning tree of *G* is a selection of edges of *G* that form a tree *spanning* every vertex. That is, every vertex lies in the tree, but no cycles (or loops) are formed. On the other hand, every bridge of *G* must belong to *T*.

It can also be defined as tree of a connected graph *G* have maximal set of edges of *G* that contains no cycle, or as a minimal set of edges that connect all vertices.

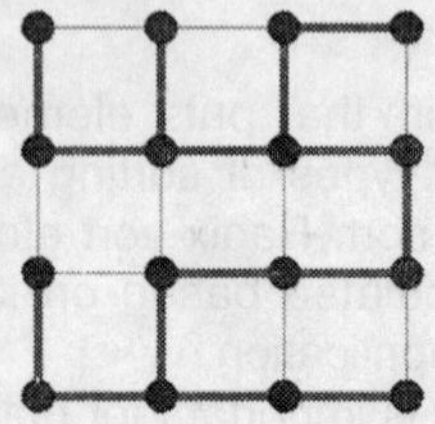

S-R Flip-Flop

This is also noted as "RS flip-flop". The "S" stands for Set while "R" stands for Reset. When activating the "S" input will switch it to one stable state and activating the "R" input will switch it to the other state. The outputs of a basic SR flip-flop change whenever its R or S inputs change appropriately.

A clocked SR flip-flop has an extra clock input which enables or disables the other two inputs. When they are disabled the outputs remain constant.

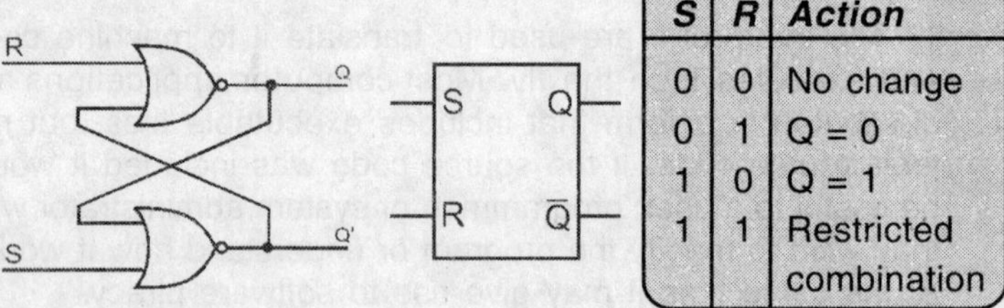

SR LATCH OPERATION		
S	***R***	***Action***
0	0	No change
0	1	Q = 0
1	0	Q = 1
1	1	Restricted combination

Stack

This is an algorithm that uses the concept of last in and first out (LIFO). This can have any abstract data type as an element but have only two fundamental operations: push and pop.

The push operation adds a new item to the top of the stack while the pop operation removes an item from the top of the stack. There are two concepts used while operating the stack—overflow and underflow. The overflow state is the state when stack is full and does not contain enough space to accept the given item. The underflow is the states when stack is empty and pop operation is assigned.

The stack top operation gets the data from the top-most position and returns it to the user without deleting it. The same underflow state can also occur in stack top operation if stack is empty.

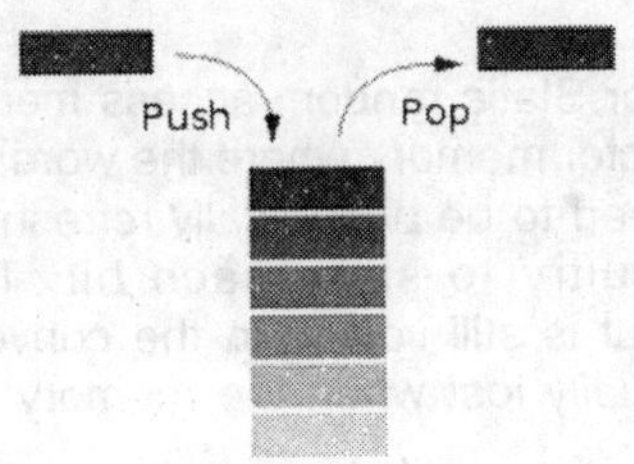

Star Network

This is a star topology where each network host is connected to a central hub with a point-to-point connection. This is the simplest network topology to implement. But there are some disadvantages of this that in case of failure of any hostage, all the networks collapse.

The network does not necessarily have to resemble a star to be classified as a star network but all of the nodes on the network must be connected to one central device.

The hub acts as a signal repeater and all traffic traverses the network passes through the central hub. An advantage of the star topology is the simplicity of adding additional nodes.

Static Data Structure

There are two types of data structure – Static data structure and Dynamic data structure.

The static data structures are designed to store static set of data. But static set of data doesn't mean that we cannot change the assigned values of elements. It is the memory size allocated to "data", which is static so that, it is possible to change content of a static structure but without increasing the memory space allocated to it.

On the other hand dynamic data structure can change the memory space according to needs like list.

Static RAM

This stands for Static random-access memory. This is a type of semiconductor memory where the word *static* indicates that it does not need to be periodically refreshed. It uses bistable latching circuitry to store each bit. This exhibits data remanence but is still *volatile* in the conventional sense that data is eventually lost when the memory is not powered.

Structured Programming

This is a programming paradigm aimed on improving the clarity, quality, and development time of a computer program by making extensive use of subroutines, block structures and for and while loops - in contrast to using simple tests and jumps such as the *goto* statement which could lead to "spaghetti code" which is both difficult to follow and to maintain.

Super Computer

This is high value computer used for big calculations like quantum physics, weather forecasting, climate research, molecular modelling as computing the structures and properties of chemical compounds, biological macromolecules, polymers, and crystals, and physical simulations such as simulation of airplanes in wind tunnels, simulation of the detonation of nuclear weapons, and research into nuclear fusion.

This was introduced in the 1960s and was designed primarily by Seymour Cray at Control Data Corporation. He then took over the supercomputer market with his new designs, holding the top spot in supercomputing for five years (1985–1990). In the 1980s a large number of smaller competitors entered the market, in parallel to the creation of the minicomputer market a decade earlier, but many of these disappeared in the mid-1990s "supercomputer market crash".

Swapping

This is a simple memory/process management technique used by the operating system to increase the utilization of the processor by moving some blocked process from the main memory to the secondary memory as hard disk. Thus forming a queue of temporarily suspended process and the execution continues with the newly arrived process.

This concept is used in several context like in programming to swap the value of two variables.

Synchronous Communication

The synchronous communication requires that each end of an exchange of communication respond in turn without initiating a new communication. A typical activity that might use a synchronous protocol would be a transmission of files from one point to another. As each transmission is received, a response is returned indicating success or the need to resend. Each successive transmission of data requires a response to the previous transmission before a new one can be initiated.

Synchronous Counter

This is a simple way of implementing the logic for counting each bit of an ascending counter. For example, bit 1 toggles when bit 0 is logic high; bit 2 toggles when both bit 1 and bit 0 are logic high; bit 3 toggles when bit 2, bit 1 and bit 0 are all high and so on. This can also be implemented with hardware finite state machines which are more complex but allow for smoother and more stable transitions.

Syntax Error

This is also known as syntactic error. This is an error in the format of a statement in a computer program that violates the rules of the programming language employed. This is most important part of compiler functioning.

System Programming

There are two types of programming—System Programming and Application Programming. System Programming refers to the architecture and design of the applications and services that make up operating system.

System Software

This is computer software designed to operate the computer hardware and to provide a platform for running application software. The basic types of system software are:

- The computer BIOS and device firmware, provides basic functionality to operate and control the hardware connected to or built into the computer.
- Utility software, which helps to analyze, configure, optimize and maintain the computer.
- The operating system (prominent examples being Microsoft Windows, Mac OS X and Linux), which allows the parts of a computer to work together by performing

tasks like transferring data between memory and disks or rendering output onto a display device. It also provides a platform to run high-level system software and application software.

Semantics

This is the study of meaning of any statement. It focuses on the relation between *signifiers*, such as words, phrases, signs and symbols, and what they stand for, their denotata. This is important part of compiler functioning. A dedicated layer is specified for semantics checking.

Serial Processing

This is a sequential processing by two or more processing units. The output of one process became input of other process. It means next process could not move till the first responded.

Silicon Diode

A crystal diode that uses silicon as a semiconductor; used as a detector in ultra-high- and super-high-frequency circuits. Also known as silicon detector.

Subnet

This is known as sub-network. This is a logically visible subdivision of an IP network. The practice of dividing a network into sub-networks is called sub-netting.

All computers that belong to a subnet are addressed with a common, identical, most-significant bit-group in their IP address. This results in the logical division of an IP address into two fields, a network or routing prefix and the rest field. The rest field is a specific identifier for the computer or the network interface.

System Log

This is a record for computer data logging. Syslog can be used for computer system management and security auditing as well as generalized informational, analysis, and debugging messages. It allows separation of the software that generates messages from the system that stores them and the software that reports and analyzes them. This can be used to integrate log data from many different types of systems into a central repository.

It also provides devices which would otherwise be unable to communicate the means to notify administrators of problems or performance.

System Analyst

They are human beings which do researches, plans solutions, recommends software and systems, and coordinates development to meet business or other requirements. They may be responsible for developing cost analysis, design considerations, and implementation time-lines.

They will be familiar with multiple variety of programming languages, operating systems, and computer hardware platforms. Because they often write user requests into technical specifications, the systems analysts are the liaisons between vendors and information technology professionals.

Sandbox

This is a testing environment which isolates untested code changes and outright experimentation from the production environment or repository in the context of software development. This protects live servers and their data and other collections of code, data and/or content, proprietary or public, from changes that could be damaging to a mission-critical system or which could simply be difficult to revert.

Sandboxes replicate at least the minimal functionality needed to accurately test the programs or other code under development e.g., usage of the same environment variables.

Servlet

This is a small j2ee program which runs on a server. The term was coined in the context of the Java applet, a small program that is sent as a separate file along with a Web (HTML) page.

Java applets usually intended for running on a client and can result in such services as performing a calculation for a user or positioning an image based on user interaction.

Set-top Box

These are used in cable television and satellite television systems to transform the signal from the cable or satellite to a form that can be used by the television set or other receiver. This is an information appliance device which generally contains a tuner and connects to a television set and an external source of signal, turning the signal into content which is then displayed on the television screen or other display device.

Spam

This is flooding with many copies of the same message over the network in an attempt to force the message on people who would not otherwise choose to receive it. Most spam is commercial advertising, often for dubious products, get-rich-quick schemes, or quasi-legal services. Spam costs the sender very little to send — most of the costs are paid for by the recipient or the carriers rather than by the sender.

Spoofing

This is the creation of TCP/IP packets using somebody else's IP address. Routers use the "destination IP" address in order to forward packets through the Internet, but ignore the "source IP" address. That address is only used by the destination machine when it responds back to the source.

SQL

This stands for Structured Query Language and is a programming language designed for managing data in relational database management systems.

This is originally based upon relational algebra and tuple relational calculus. This facilitates data insert, query, update and delete, schema creation and modification, and data access control.

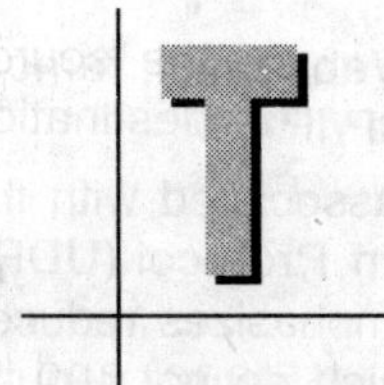

Tautology

This is a technique to say the same thing by using different words even if the repetition does not provide clarity. This is a series of self-reinforcing statements which cannot be disproved because the statements depend on the assumption that they are already correct.

For example, I could say "I am going to the study", which may be true or false. "I am not going to the study" is equally likely to be true or false.

"I am going to the study AND I am not going to the study" is logically false, because contradictory statements cannot be simultaneously true in logic.

"I am going to the study OR I am not going to the study" is always true, however, because either one statement or the other must be true. Therefore, it is a tautology.

TCP

This stands for Transmission Control Protocol used in data communication. This is one of the core protocols of the Internet Protocol Suite. The entire suite is commonly referred to as *TCP/IP*.

This provides reliable and ordered delivery of a stream of bytes or packets from one computer or electronic devices to another computer or electronic devices. Major Internet applications such as the World Wide Web, email, remote administration and file transfer rely on TCP/IP.

There are other protocols which are associated with the data communication like User Datagram Protocol (UDP), which provides a datagram service and emphasizes reduced latency over reliability. This is used which do not require reliable data stream service.

TDM

This stands for Time Division Multiplexing. This is a way of multiplexing where two or more bit streams or signals are transferred apparently simultaneously as sub-channels in one communication channel but are physically taking turns on the channel.

The time is divided into several recurrent time-slots of fixed length assigning one for each sub-channel. The data block of sub-channel 1 is transmitted during timeslot 1, data block of sub-channel 2 during timeslot 2, so on. It also consists synchronization channel and sometimes error correction channel before the synchronization.

After the last sub-channel, error correction, and synchronization, the cycle starts all over again with a new frame starting with the second data block from sub-channel 1 begins.

Teleconferncing

This means meeting between two units through a telecommunications medium. This may be audio based, video base or both. It is a generic term for linking people between two or more locations by electronics devices. This gives the sense of physical presence of human beings during conferencing even when there are no such existence. There are at least six types of teleconferencing: audio, audio graphic, computer, video, business television (BTV), and distance education.

Telnet

This is a network protocol used for local area networks or internet to provide a bidirectional interactive text-oriented communication facility using a virtual terminal connection. User data is interspersed in-band with Telnet control information in an 8-bit byte oriented data connection over the Transmission Control Protocol (TCP).

Templet

This is a page created to be included in other pages. This usually contain repetitive material which might need to show up on any number of articles or pages. They are commonly used for boilerplate messages, standard warnings or notices, info boxes, navigational boxes and similar purposes. This is used in mobile and mailing to keep as signature of user. Even during page designing this is used to show different fixed entities.

Ten's Complement

Complement arithmetic offers a simple and elegant method for performing addition and subtraction on computer. Signed integers are usually stored on the computer in complement form and can be used in this form directly in arithmetic expression. The ten's-complement of any digit is the number we would need to make the number a 10. For example, if we had the number 7, we would need 3 more to make it a 10. So 3 is the ten's-complement of 7, and 7 is the ten's-complement of 3.

The other way to obtain 10's complement is first get 9's complement of each digit and then add 1 to final result.

Example:10's complement of 56 is:

First take 9's complement of each digit—

9 – 5 = 4 and 9 – 6 = 3 ; 9's complement is equal to 43.

10's complement is 43 + 1 = 44.

T-Flip-Flop

This is a form of J-K Flip-flop where J and K both inputs become same. This is viewed as:

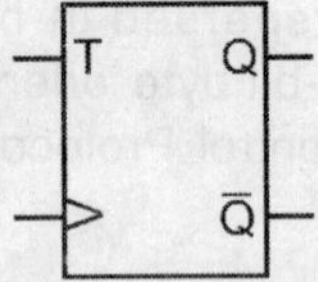

If the T input is high, it changes state. If the T input is low, it holds the previous value. This behaviour is described by the characteristic equation:

$$Q_{next} = T \oplus Q = T\overline{Q} + \overline{T}Q$$

This can be described in a truth table as :

T flip-flop operation							
Characteristic table				***Excitation table***			
T	***Q***	Q_{next}	**Comment**	***Q***	Q_{next}	***T***	**Comment**
0	0	0	hold state (no clk)	0	0	0	No change
0	1	1	hold state (no clk)	1	1	0	No change
1	0	1	toggle	0	1	1	Complement
1	1	0	toggle	1	0	1	Complement

Thrashing

This refers to two or more processes accessing a shared resource repeatedly such that serious system performance degradation occurs because the system is spending a disproportionate amount of time just *accessing* the shared resource. This is a situation where large amounts of computer resources are used to do a minimal amount of work which leads to resource contention.

Once started, thrashing is typically self-sustaining until something occurs to remove the original situation that led to the initial thrashing behaviour. This is often the case when a CPU can process more information than can be held in available RAM;

Threading

This is the execution of thread which is a small utility software programme. Thread is the smallest unit of processing that can be scheduled by an operating system. The implementation of threads and processes differs from one operating system to another. Multiple threads can exist within the same process and share resources such as memory while different processes do not share these resources. It can be represented as:

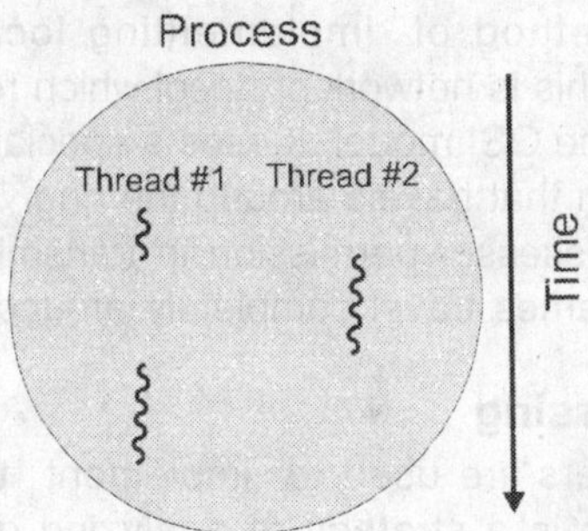

Multithreading is used in modern computer systems. There are different types of multithreading—Block multi-threading, Interleaved multi-threading, Simultaneous multi-threading.

Time Complexity

This quantifies the amount of time taken by an algorithm to run as a function of the size of the input to the problem. This is commonly expressed using Big O notation. When expressed this way, the time complexity is said to be described *asymptotically*, i.e., as the input size goes to infinity.

For example, if the time required by an algorithm on all inputs of size n is at most $5n^3 + 3n$, the asymptotic time complexity is $O(n^3)$.

Time Slicing

This is a scheduling technique used in operating system. This is the most common technique to implement multitasking in operating systems. Here each process is assigned a fixed time. This is not a good technique because whenever large time is assigned to a process, it is wastage of time.

Token Ring

This is a method of implementing local area network technology. This is network protocol which resides at the data link layer of the OSI model. It uses a special three-byte frame called a token that travels around the ring. Token-possession grants the possessor permission to transmit on the medium. Token ring frames travel completely around the loop.

Top-Down Parsing

The LL parsers are used to implement top-down parsing strategy. This is a strategy of analyzing data relationships by hypothesizing parse tree structures and then considering whether the fundamental structures are compatible with the hypothesis. This is a parsing strategy where one first looks at the highest level of the parse tree and works down the parse tree by using the rewriting rules of a formal grammar.

It occurs in the analysis of both natural languages and languages. This can be used as an attempt to find left-most derivations of an input-stream by searching for parse-trees using a top-down expansion of the given formal grammar rules. Tokens are consumed from left to right.

Simple implementations of top-down parsing do not terminate for left-recursive grammars. With backtracking top down parsing may have exponential time complexity with respect to the length of the input for ambiguous CFGs. However, more sophisticated top-down parsers have been created by Frost, Hafiz, and Callaghan which do accommodate ambiguity and left recursion in polynomial time and which generate polynomial-sized representations of the potentially-exponential number of parse trees.

Topology

It emerged through the development of concepts from geometry and set theory, such as space, dimension, and transformation. This is a major area of mathematics concerned with properties that are preserved under continuous deformations of objects, such as deformations that involve stretching, but no tearing or gluing.

Transducer

This commonly implies the use of a sensor. Transducers are widely used in measuring instruments. This is an electronic equipment which converts one type of energy to another. Energy types include electrical, mechanical, electro-magnetic (including light), chemical, acoustic or thermal energy.

Transient Error

This is an error that occurs once or at unpredictable intervals.

Transistor

This is a semiconductor electronic device used to amplify and switch electronic signals and power. This is formed of a semiconductor material with at least three terminals for connection to an external circuit. A voltage or current applied to one pair of the transistor's terminals changes the current flowing through another pair of terminals. This could be burnt when excess heat is generated due to high voltage.

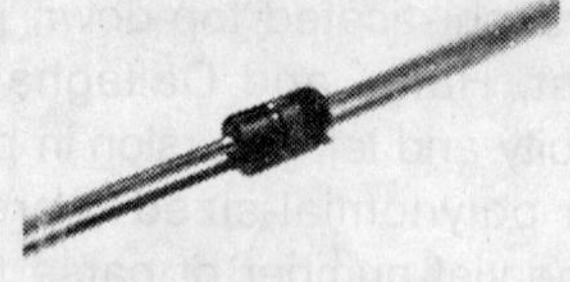

Transistor-Transistor Logic

This is famous as TTL and belongs to digital circuits built from bipolar junction transistors (BJT) and resistors. TTL is notable for being a widespread integrated circuit (IC) family used in many applications such as computers, industrial controls, test equipment and instrumentation, consumer electronics, synthesizers, etc.

Transistor are used for amplifying purpose. Since amplifying function are performed by TTL by combining the characteristics of two transistors.

Transport Layer

This is layer 4 of Open Systems Interconnection(OSI) model of computer networking and provides end-to-end communication services for applications within a layered architecture of network components and protocols. This provides convenient services such as connection-oriented data stream support, reliability, flow control, and multiplexing.

Such layers are also present in the TCP/IP model but the definitions of the transport layer are slightly different in this. The TCP/IP model is largely for a convenient application programming interface to internet hosts as opposed to the OSI-model definition of the transport layer.

Tree

This is an algorithm used in data structure used for storing and searching the data. There are several types of tree present in data structure like Binary Tree, ordered tree, unordered tree. There are several tree traversing algorithm present. This can be represented as:

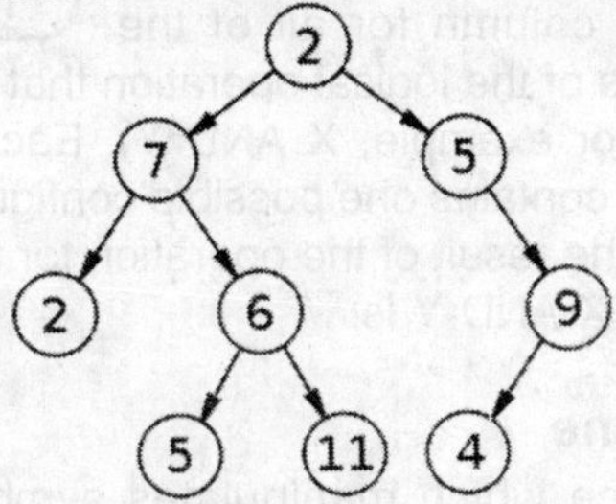

Trojan Horse

It can also simply pronounced as Trojan. It behaves like a virus. This is a computer software which appears to perform a desirable function for the user prior to run or install but steals information or harms the system Once it has been installed on a target computer system a hacker may have access to the computer remotely and perform various operations.

Trojan horses, in this way require interaction with a hacker to fulfil their purpose, though the hacker need not be the individual responsible for distributing the Trojan horse. It is possible for individual hackers to scan computers on a network using a port scanner in the hope of finding one with a malicious Trojan horse installed, which the hacker can then use to control the target computer.

Truth Table

This is a logical table specifically used in connection with Boolean algebra, Boolean functions, and propositional calculus to compute the functional values of logical expressions on each of their functional arguments.

Practically, a truth table is composed of one column for each input variable (for example, X and Y), and one final column for all of the possible results of the logical operation that the table is meant to represent (for example, X AND Y). Each row of the truth table therefore contains one possible configuration of the input variables and the result of the operation for those values. e.g., Truth table for X AND Y is:

Inputs		Outputs
X	***Y***	***S***
0	0	0
1	0	0
0	1	0
1	1	1

Turning Machine

This is a device which manipulates symbols on a strip of tape according to a table of rules. This can be used to simulate the logic of any computer algorithm and particularly useful in explaining the functions of a CPU inside a computer. This is not intended as a practical computing technology but rather as a hypothetical device representing a computing machine. Turing machines help computer scientists understand the limits of mechanical computation.

Two's Complement

Complement arithmetic offers a simple and elegant method for performing addition and subtraction on computer. Signed integers are usually stored on the computer in complement form and can be used in this form directly in arithmetic expression.

This is a system in which negative numbers are represented. This system is the most common method of representing signed integers on computers.

The two's complement of a binary number is defined as the value obtained by subtracting the number from a large power of two.

It can also be calculated as first taking the one's complemented finally add 1. An N-bit two's-complement numeral system can represent every integer in the range -2^{N-1} to $2^{N-1} - 1$.

Third Generation Computer

Use of transistors were great deal of improvement over the vacuum tubes while developing the computer. But transistors generate heat and damage the sensitive areas of the computer. It may also lead to loss of machine.

To eradicate this problem, an Integrated circuit was invented in 1958 by Jack Kilby. It combined electronic components onto a small silicon disc made up from quartz. More advancement made possible the fittings of even more components on a small chip or a semi conductor. This gave the birth of third generation computers. The operating system allowed the machines to run many different applications.

Threshold Gate

This is an electronic device that performs a threshold operation. Threshold is the limit over which any instrument destroyes.

Thyristor

This is a solid-state semiconductor electronic device having four layers of alternating N-type and P-type material. They are used as bistable switches when their gate receive a current trigger and continue to conduct while they are forward biased.

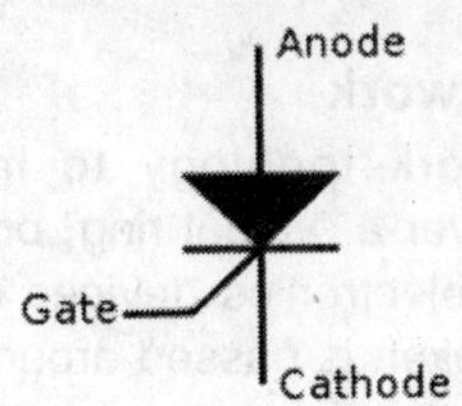

Transponder

There are several meanings of the transponder like:

- An automatic device that receives, amplifies, and retransmits a signal on a different frequency.
- A receiver-transmitter that will generate a reply signal upon proper electronic interrogation.
- An automatic device that transmits a predetermined message in response to a predefined received signal.

Triode

This is an electronic amplification device having three active electrodes. This is commonly applies to a vacuum tube with three elements: the filament or cathode, the grid, and the plate or anode. The triode vacuum tube was the first electronic amplification device.

Truncation Error

This is also known as local truncation error. This is rounding off the number. This is an error made by numerical algorithms that arises from taking finite number of steps in computation. It is present even with infinite-precision arithmetic, because it is caused by truncation of the infinite Taylor series to form the algorithm.

Use of arbitrarily small steps in numerical computation is prevented by round-off error, which are the consequence of using finite precision floating point numbers on computers.

Token Bus Network

This is network topology to implementing the token ring protocol over a "virtual ring" on a coaxial cable. Several computers or electronics devices are networked through a main wire. A token is passed around the network nodes and only the node possessing the token may transmit. If a node doesn't have anything to send, the token is passed on to the next node on the virtual ring. Each node must know the address of its neighbour in the ring, so a special protocol is needed to notify the other nodes of connections to, and disconnections from, the ring.

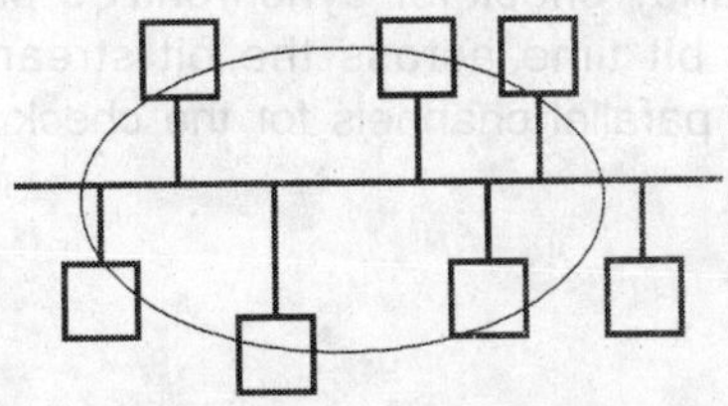

Touch screen

This is the latest invention in the field of communication. This is an electronic visual display that can detect the presence and location of a touch within the display area. The term generally refers to touching the display of the device with a finger. Touch screens can also sense other passive objects like a stylus, joy stick etc. This is common in devices such as all-in-one computers, tablet computers, and smartphones. The simplicity and convenient use of touch screen devices has enhanced their demand.

There are two layers in touch screen monitors. First one is the sensor which takes inputs from the users while second one is main media which do the action.

This has two main attributes. First, it enables one to interact directly with what is displayed, rather than indirectly with a pointer controlled by a mouse or touchpad. Secondly, it lets one do so without requiring any intermediate device that would need to be held in the hand. Such displays can be attached to computers, or to networks as terminals. They also play a prominent role in the design of digital appliances such as the personal digital assistant (PDA), satellite navigation devices, mobile phones, and video games.

Transverse Redundancy Check

This is also known as vertical redundancy check. This is a redundancy check for synchronized parallel bits applied once per bit time across the bit streams. This requires additional parallel channels for the check bit or bits.

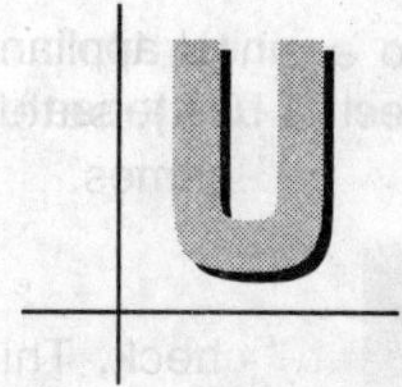

Unary Operation

This is a mathematical operation which has only one operand, i.e., a single input. Specifically, it is a function

$$f : A \to A$$

where A is a set. In this case f is called a unary operation on A.

This is opposite to binary operation. Common notations of unary operation are prefix notation, postfix notation, functional notation and superscripts. Other notations exist as well, for example, in the case of the square root a horizontal bar over the argument extending the square root sign can indicate the extent of the argument.

Underflow

This is a condition in which an attempt is made to read an empty buffer. It means there is nothing stored in buffer or memory.

Unibus

This is one of the earliest computer bus technologies used with PDP-11 and VAX systems. This is manufactured by the Digital Equipment Corporation (DEC) of Maynard, Massachusetts and developed around 1969 by Gordon Bell and Harold McFarland.

This is composed of 72 wires (2 connectors x 36 lines per connector). It could exist within a backplane or on a cable.

Up to 20 devices could be connected to a single Unibus segment. For additional segments to connect a bus repeater are used.

The design deliberately minimized the amount of redundant logic required in the system. For example, a system always contained more slave devices than master devices so most of the fancy logic required to implement asynchronous data transfers was forced into the relatively few master devices.

Unipolar Signal

This is also called unipolar transmission. This is a baseband method of sending binary data over wire or cable. The digits 0 and 1 are used to indicate two logic states—low and high respectively.

The illustration shows a unipolar signal as it might appear on the screen of an oscilloscope. where each horizontal division represents one bit. The logic 0 state is approximately 0 volts while logic 1 is approximately +5 volts. Alternatively, logic 0 might be approximately +5 volts, and logic 1 might be approximately 0 volts.

Unit Matrix

This is also known as the identity matrix. It is denoted by I_n, or simply by I if the size is immaterial or can be trivially determined by the context. There are ones on the main diagonal and zeros elsewhere in $n \times n$ square matrix.

For Example:

$$I_1 = [1],\ I_2 = \begin{bmatrix} 1 & 0 \\ 0 & 1 \end{bmatrix},\ I_3 = \begin{bmatrix} 1 & 0 & 0 \\ 0 & 1 & 0 \\ 0 & 0 & 1 \end{bmatrix},\ ....,\ I_n = \begin{bmatrix} 1 & 0 & \cdots & 0 \\ 0 & 1 & \cdots & 0 \\ \vdots & \vdots & \ddots & \vdots \\ 0 & 0 & \cdots & 1 \end{bmatrix}$$

Unit Testing

This is a testing method by which individual units of source code are tested to determine there correctness for use. The big codes are divided into several functions and each functions are tested individually. A unit is the smallest testable part of a programme. Unit tests are created by programmers or occasionally by white box testers during the development process. In object-oriented programming a unit is often an entire interface, such as a class, but could be an individual method.

Each test case is independent from the others and tested separately. Unit tests are typically written and run by software developers to ensure that code meets its design and behaves as intended. Its implementation can vary from being very manual to being formalized as part of build automation.

There are many unit testing tools are available in market like — PMD.

Universal Turing Machine

This is a Turing machine which can simulate an arbitrary Turing machine on arbitrary input. Alan Turing introduced this machine in 1936–1937. Such machine achieves this by reading both the description of the machine—to be simulated as well as the input thereof from its own tape.

It is considered that this model is one of the origin of the stored program computer which was used by John von Neumann.

UNIX

It is the multitasking, multi-user computer operating system originally developed in 1969 by a group of AT&T employees at Labs. The scholars involved were Ken Thompson, Dennis Ritchie, Brian Kernighan, Douglas McIlroy, and Joe Ossanna. It was first developed in language. Today's Unix system evolution is split into various branches, developed over time by AT&T as well as various commercial vendors, universities and non-profit organizations.

Under-modulation

This is the condition in which the peak values of the modulating signal stay for a long period of time well below the maximum value permitted by the transmission system or equipment considered.

UPS

This stands for uninterruptible power supply and also known as uninterruptible power source or battery/flywheel backup. This is an electrical apparatus which provides emergency power to a load when the input power source, typically mains power fails. This is different from an emergency power system because it will provide instantaneous or near-instantaneous protection from input power interruptions by means of one or more attached batteries and associated electronic circuitry for low power users. The on-battery runtime of most uninterruptible power sources is relatively short—5–15 minutes being typical for smaller units—but sufficient to allow time to bring an auxiliary power source on line, or to properly shut down the protected equipment.

This is essential part of computer setup because computer need proper shutdown and start while operating. In the starting process, computer loads several files to start properly and similarly unstores files during shutdown. If power supply is interrupted during the process, it leads to abnormal shutdown. So there is need of such device which can provide uninterrupted power supply; which could be achieved by UPS.

UDP

This stands for User Datagram Protocol and is one of the core members of the Suite. There is no need of setting dedicated communication channel before sending the data. The protocol was designed by David in 1980.

The messages sent by computer applications while using UDP are known as datagrams. This is achieved to other hosts on an Internet Protocol (IP) network without requiring prior communications to set up like, special transmission channels or data paths.

This provides an unreliable service and datagram may arrive out of order, appear duplicated, or go missing without notice. This assumes that error checking and correction is either not necessary or performed in the application and avoiding the overhead of such processing at the network interface level. Time-sensitive applications often use UDP because dropping packets is preferable to waiting for delayed packets, which may not be an option in a real-time system.

The Transmission Control Protocol (TCP) or Stream Control Transmission Protocol (SCTP) are used during data communication when there is need of error correction.

UID

This stands for User interface design. The goal of user interface design is to make the user's interaction simple and efficient as much as possible, in terms of accomplishing user goals.

This is often called design. This is helpful for computers, appliances, machines, mobile communication devices, software applications, and websites with the focus on the users' experience and interaction.

Graphic design may be utilized to support its usability. The design process must balance technical functionality and visual elements to create a system that is not only operational but also usable and adaptable to the changing user needs. Good user interface design facilitates finishing the task at hand without drawing unnecessary attention to itself.

Unicode

This is standard for the consistent encoding, representation and handling of text expressed in most of the world's systems. This is used to convert different letters and digits in particular code named Unicode.

This is developed in conjunction with the Universal Character Set standard and published in book form as the Unicode Standard. The latest version of Unicode consists of more than 109,000 characters covering 93 scripts, an encoding methodology and set of standard character encodings, an enumeration of character properties such as upper and lower case, etc. As of 2011, the most recent major revision of Unicode is Unicode 6.0.

URL

This stands for uniform resource locator or universal resource locator. This is a specific character string which constitutes a reference to an Internet resource.

Every website is identified by a URL which is unique. This is written in digital form but for convenience, it is viewed as strings. For example, the actual URL is 4045://120.23.12 but it could be seen as www.rameshpublishinghouse.com.

❑❑❑

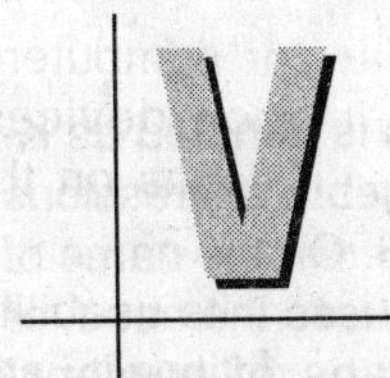

VDU

This stands for Visual Display Unit. This is an older British term used to describe a visual display device for a computer like a flat panel display, monitor, and a projector. This is most commonly used to describe a standard CRT monitor.

Vector Processing

This is associated with the concept of a "supercomputer". This is an architectural technique for achieving high performance. The origins of vector processing lay in trying to address the problem of instruction bandwidth. It was possible to build multiple pipelined functional units but the fetch and decode of instructions from memory was too slow. Applying a single instruction to multiple data elements is one simple and logical way to leverage limited instruction bandwidth.

The most powerful computers of the 1970s and 1980s tended to be vector machines but with increasingly higher degrees of semiconductor integration the mismatch between instruction bandwidth and operand bandwidth essentially went away.

The SIMD approach has been applied to the processing of 8 and 16-bit multimedia data by 32 and 64-bit processors. Under the names "MMX" and "SSE", SIMD processing can be found in essentially every modern personal computer, where it is exploited by image processing and audio applications.

Veith Diagram

This is also known as f Karnaugh Map. This is denoted as K-map. This is method to simplify Boolean algebra expressions and developed by Maurice Karnaugh in 1953. On the name of inventor it is known as Karnaugh Map. It reduces the need for extensive calculations by taking advantage of humans' pattern-recognition capability and permitting the rapid identification and elimination of potential race conditions.

It is represented into rectangular fashion as binary digits in the map represent the function's output for any given combination of inputs. So 0 is written in the upper leftmost corner of the map because $f = 0$ when $A = 0$, $B = 0$, $C = 0$, $D = 0$. Similarly we mark the bottom right corner as 1 because $A = 1$, $B = 0$, $C = 1$, $D = 0$ gives $f = 1$. Note that the values are ordered in a Gray code, so that precisely one variable changes between any pair of adjacent cells.

The Boolean variables are transferred generally from a truth table and ordered according to the principles of Gray code in which only one variable change in between adjacent squares is desirable. Once the table is generated and the output possibilities are transcribed, the data is arranged into the largest possible groups containing 2^n cells (n=0,1,2,3...).The minterm is generated through the axiom laws of Boolean algebra. The following is an unsimplified Boolean Algebra function with Boolean variables *A, B, C, D*, and their inverses. They can be represented in two different notations with the values inside $\sum$ are as mid terms to map.

These are with input A,B,C,D:

$f(A,B,C,D) = \sum(5, 6, 7, 8, 9, 10, 11, 12)$

and

$$f(A,B,C,D)=(\bar{A}BC\bar{D})+(\bar{A}\bar{B}\bar{C}\bar{D})+(A\bar{B}\bar{C}D)+(A\bar{B}C\bar{D})+$$
$$(A\bar{B}CD)+(AB\bar{C}\bar{D})+$$

Using the defined mid terms, the truth table can be shown as:

#	*A*	*B*	*C*	*D*	*f (A,B,C,D)*
0	0	0	0	0	0
1	0	0	0	1	0
2	0	0	1	0	0
3	0	0	1	1	0
4	0	1	0	0	0
5	0	1	0	1	0
6	0	1	1	0	1
7	0	1	1	1	0
8	1	0	0	0	1
9	1	0	0	1	1
10	1	0	1	0	1
11	1	0	1	1	1
12	1	1	0	0	1
13	1	1	0	1	1
14	1	1	1	0	1
15	1	1	1	1	0

The input variables can be combined in 16 different ways. That is why the Karnaugh map has 16 positions and is arranged in a 4 × 4 grid. The map is represented as:

CD \ AB	00	01	11	10
00	0	4	12	8
01	1	5	13	9
11	3	7	15	11
10	2	6	14	10

ABCD	ABCD
0000 - 0	1000 - 8
0001 - 1	1001 - 9
0010 - 2	1010 - 10
0011 - 3	1011 - 11
0100 - 4	1100 - 12
0101 - 5	1101 - 13
0110 - 6	1110 - 14
0111 - 7	1111 - 15

Verification & Validation

The Verification is a quality control process which is used to evaluate whether a product, service, or system complies with regulations, specifications, or conditions imposed at the start of a development phase. It can be in development, scale-up, or production. This is generally an internal process.

On the other hand Validation is a quality assurance process of establishing evidence which provides a high degree of assurance that a product, service, or system accomplishes its intended requirements. This often involves acceptance of fitness for purpose with end users and other product stakeholders. This is often an external process.

Virtual Circuit

This is synonymous with virtual connection as well as channel. This is a connection oriented communication service that is delivered by means of packet or frame mode communication. After a connection, a virtual circuit is established between two nodes or application processes. The bit of data flow could occur after the connection. A virtual circuit protocol allows higher level protocols to avoid dealing with the division of data into segments, packets, or frames.

The communication in virtual circuit resembles to circuit switching since both are connection oriented.

Virtual Machine

This is a software implementation of a machine which executes programs like a physical machine. This is separated into two major categories based on their use and degree of correspondence to any real machine.

There are two types of virtual machines—System Virtual Machine and Process Virtual Machine. A system virtual machine provides a complete system platform which supports the execution of a complete operating system while a process virtual machine is designed to run a single program. An essential characteristic of a virtual machine is that the software running inside is limited to the resources and abstractions provided by the virtual machine—it cannot break out of its virtual world.

Virtual machine like, Java Virtual machine are most popular which gives support to Java programming.

Virtual Memory

This is a memory management technique developed for multitasking kernels. This shows the presence of memory to processor but in reality, there is no such memory. This technique virtualizes a computer architecture's various forms of computer data storage like random-access memory and disk storage, allowing a program to be designed as though there is only one kind of memory, "virtual" memory, which behaves like directly addressable read/write memory (RAM).

VLSI

This stands for **V**ery-**L**arge-**S**cale **I**ntegration. This is the process of creating integrated circuits by combining thousands of transistors into a single chip. The microprocessor is an example VLSI device.

It began in the 1970s when complex semiconductors and communication technologies were being developed. Initially there were two transistors present in a chip. Subsequent advances added more and more transistors and systems were integrated over time.

But improvement in technique and Small-Scale Integration (SSI) led to devices with hundreds of logic gates known as Medium-Scale Integration (MSI). Further improve-ments led to Large-Scale Integration (LSI) which consisted systems with at least a thousand logic gates. Current technology has moved far past this mark and today's microprocessors have many millions of gates and billions of individual transistors.

At one time, there was an effort to name and calibrate various levels of large-scale integration above VLSI. Terms like **U**ltra-**L**arge-**S**cale **I**ntegration (ULSI) were used. But the huge number of gates and transistors available on common devices has rendered such fine distinctions moot. Terms suggesting greater than VLSI levels of integration are no longer in widespread use.

Volatile Memory

This is computer memory which requires power to maintain the stored information. In contrast to this, non-volatile memory does not require a maintained power supply. It has been popularly known as temporary memory. This is main memory of computer. Whenever any machine starts, it first loads data in main memory to operate.

The random access memory (RAM) is classical example of volatile memory. The other examples are dynamic random access memory (DRAM), static random access memory (SRAM) etc.

Von Neumann Machine

This is the basic design of the modern or classical computer. The concept was fully articulated by three principal scientists involved in the construction of ENIAC during World War II—Arthur Burks, Herman Goldstine, and John Von Neumann in "Preliminary Discussion of the Logical Design of an Electronic Computing **I**nstrument" (1946). Although many researchers contributed ideas directly or indirectly to the paper, Von Neumann was the principal author and it is frequently cited as the birth certificate of computer science.

V-band

The electromagnetic spectrum ranges of V-band is ranging from 50 to 75 GHz. The V band is not heavily used except for millimeter wave radar research and other kinds of scientific research. It should not be confused with the 600–1000 MHz range of Band-V (band-five) of the UHF frequency range.

Virus

This is a program or piece of code which is loaded into computer without the knowledge of user and runs against wishes of user. Viruses replicate themselves. A simple virus that can make a copy of itself over and over again is relatively easy to produce. All computer viruses are man-made.

Even a simple virus is dangerous because it will quickly use all available memory and bring the system to a halt. An even more dangerous type of virus is the one capable of transmitting itself across networks and bypassing security systems.

There are several antivirus programs available in market since 1987, when virus infected ARPANET. These programs periodically check your computer system for the best-known types of viruses. It is suggested to regularly update the antivirus or even better to use latest antivirus to tackle the newer type of viruses.

Virus like Trojan horse is very common in computer.

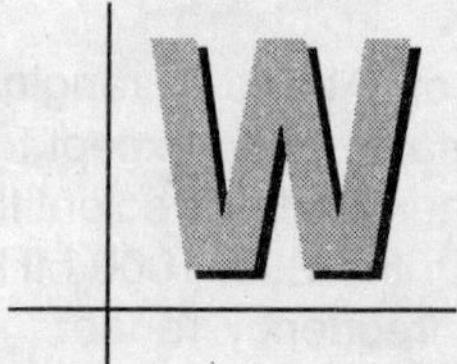

WAN

This stands for Wide Area Network. This is a telecommunication network that covers a broad area like, links across metropolitan, regional, or national boundaries. To relay data among employees, clients, buyers, and suppliers from various geographical locations Business and government entities utilize this. This supports Local Area Network and Metropolitan Area Network.

In essence this mode of telecommunication allows a business to effectively carry out its daily function regardless of location. The network of WAN can be understood by the diagram:

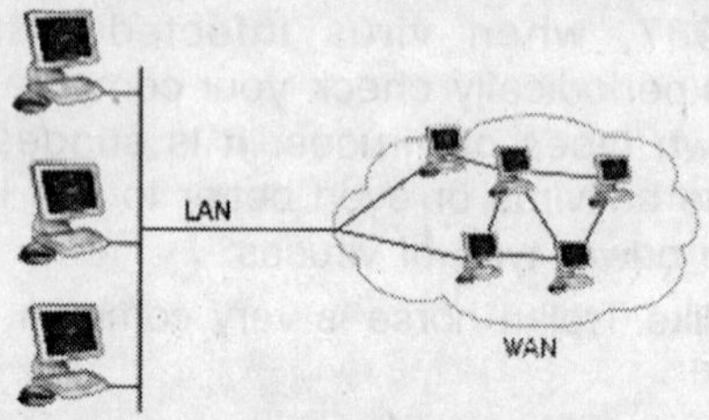

Weighted Code

This is a method of representing a decimal digit by a combination of bits in which each bit is assigned a weight and the value of the decimal digit is found by multiplying each bit by its weight and then summing the results.

Window

First time Microsoft introduced an operating environment named Windows in 1985 in response to the growing interest in graphical user interfaces. Currently Windows has approximately 82.50% of the market share of the client operating systems according to usage share of operating systems. The latest client version of Windows is Windows 7, Vista etc. While the most recent server version is Windows Server 2008 R2. This simplified the use of computer access. The origin of windows goes to a computer scientist Chase Bishop. The shell of Windows 1.0 was a program known as the MS-DOS Executive. Other supplied programs with this were Calculator, Calendar, Card file, Clipboard viewer, Clock, Control Panel, Notepad, Paint, Terminal, and Write.

Now a day's mobile are also equipped with internet facilities. They are also operated by an operating system. The most recent mobile version is Windows Phone 7, Android etc.

Web Browser

This is a software application for retrieving, presenting, and traversing information resources on the World Wide Web. The information resource is identified with the help of a Uniform Resource Identifier (URI).

Hyperlinks present in resources enable users easily to navigate their browsers to related resources. There are several Web Browsers present in the market like internet explorer, Mozilla, Google Crome, Opera etc. Any user can communicate with server in client-server architecture with the help of web browser.

Web Client

This refers to operations performed by the client in a client–server relationship in a computer network. The client is a computer application like a web browser which runs on a user's local computer or workstation and connects to a server.

There are several operations which may be performed on client-side because they require access to information or functionality that is available on the client but not on the server. Additionally, if operations can be performed by the client without sending data over the network they may take less time, use less bandwidth, and incur a lesser security risk. When the server serves data in a commonly used manner, for example, according to the HTTP or FTP protocols, users may have their choice of a number of client programs (most modern web browsers can request and receive data using both of those protocols). In the case of more specialized applications, programmers may write their own server, client, and communications protocol, that can only be used with one another.

The functions occurred at client side are keeping cookies, authenticating the user etc.

Web Designer

Web designing is the process of planning and creating a website. The person Involved in web designing is known as web designer. They design the page and flow of page. Text, images, digital media and interactive elements are used by web designers to produce the page seen on the web browser. They utilize mark-up language generally, HTML for structure and CSS for presentation as well as JavaScript to add interactivity to develop pages that can be read by web browsers. There are several others page designing technologies exits but the base of all is HTML.

Web Link

Web Link is one of the two free API's (JLink being the other) provided by PTC to create Pro/Engineer applications. According to PTC's documentation, Web Link is a JavaScript based library for use within the embedded web browser.

Web Page

This is an electronic page. This is a document of information resource suitable for the World Wide Web and can be accessed through a web browser and displayed on a monitor or mobile device. This information is usually in HTML or XHTML format, and may provide navigation to other web pages via hypertext links. Web pages frequently subsume other resources such as style sheets, scripts and images into their final presentation.

Web server

This is the combination of the hardware (the computer) and the software (the computer application) which helps to deliver content. This can be accessed through the Internet. This is the back part of client-server architecture. The primary function of a web server is to deliver web pages on request, to clients. This means delivery of HTML documents and any additional content that may be included by a document, such as images, style sheets and scripts.

Currently, all big organisations and government have there own servers which keeps information about their establishments. The use of servers has reduced the distance of world as well as simplified the work of human beings.

Web TV

This is known as Web television or Internet television or Catch-up TV. This is an emerging generation of digital entertainment which is distinct from traditional broadcast television. Delivered originally online via broadband and mobile networks.

Welcome Page

This refers to the initial or main web page of a web site. This is also called the **front page** with analogy with newspapers. It is often the index.html page at the root directory of a web site. The welcome page appears on the client side on client-server architecture whenever user hits the server. There may be more than one welcome page residing on server. The welcome page can be customized by setting of web browser.

WWW

This stands for World Wide Web. This is also written as W3. This is a system of interlinked hypertext documents accessed via the Internet. With the help of a web browser, one can view web pages that may contain text, images, videos, and other multimedia and navigate between them via hyperlinks.

WORM

This stands for Write Once Read Many. These are one time writable devices.

X.25

It was originally defined by the International Telegraph and Telephone Consultative Committee in a series of drafts and finalized in a publication known as *The Orange Book* in 1976. This is an ITU-T standard protocol used in packet switched wide area network (WAN) communication.

An X.25 WAN consists of packet-switching exchange nodes as the networking hardware and leased lines while Plain old telephone service connections or ISDN connections as physical links.

This protocol was popular during the 1980s within telecommunications companies and in financial transaction systems such as automated teller machines. It has been to a large extent replaced by less complex protocols like Internet protocol (IP). It is still used and available in niche and legacy applications.

XMOdem

This is a simple file transfer protocol developed by Ward Christensen in 1977. This became extremely popular in the early bulletin board system market because of its simplicity in implementation. But it was fairly inefficient with the speed of data communication. As modem speeds increased, this problem led to the development of a number of modified versions of XMODEM to improve performance or address other problems with the protocol. A scholar Chuck Forsberg solved the issues by inventing YMODEM protocol. But this was also not able to solve the problem effectively. It finally lead to the invention of ZMODEM protocol.

X Window System

This is also known as X11 system. This is a computer software system and network protocol which provides a basis for graphical user interfaces (GUIs). X is an architecture-independent system for remote graphical user interfaces and rich input device capabilities which allows many people to share the processing power of a time-sharing computer and to collaborate with each other through client applications running on remote computers.

It creates a hardware abstraction layer where software is used as generalized set of commands allowing for device independence and reuse of programs on any computer that implements X.

Each person using a networked terminal has the ability to interact with the display with any type of user input device. Due to the ubiquity of support for X software on Unix, Linux and Mac OS X, X is commonly used to run client applications on personal computers even when there is no need for time-sharing.

❑❑❑

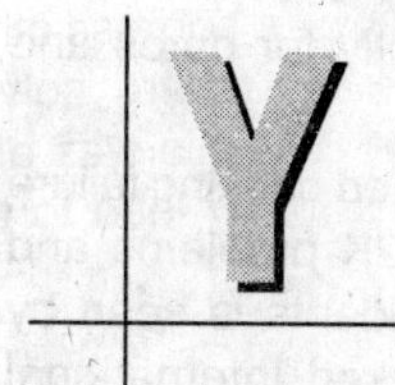

Yale Virus

This is also known as Alameda Virus, Merritt Virus, Peking Virus and Seoul Virus. This is a computer virus which infects the diskette boot sector. The virus is loaded into memory by booting from an infected disk and then infects diskettes when ALT-CTRL-DELETE is pressed. There are several anti viruses present in market to check the virus infection.

YModem

This is a protocol used for file transfer between modems. It was formally given the name "YMODEM" in 1985 by Ward Christensen but developed by Chuck Forsberg. This was the successor to XMODEM and MODEM7. This was first implemented by him in his CP/M *YAM* program. The ZModem replaced the YModem.

Y2K

This is known as Year 2000 problem, the Millennium bug or the Y2K bug. This was the problem for both digital and non-digital documentation in data storage situations which resulted from the practice of abbreviating a four-digit year to two digits.

In computer programs, the practice of representing the year with two digits became problematic with logical errors arising upon "rollover" from xx99 to xx00. This lead to some date-related processing to operate incorrectly for dates and times on and after January 1, 2000.

There is evidence of at least one date-related banking failure due to Y2K. There were plenty of other Y2K problems and that none of the glitches caused major incidents is seen by some, such as the Director of the UN-backed International Y2K Co-operation Centre and the head of the UK's Taskforce 2000, as vindication of the Y2K preparation. However, some questioned whether the relative absence of computer failures was the result of the preparation undertaken or whether the significance of the problem had been overstated.

❑ ❑ ❑

Z

Zmodem

This is a file transfer protocol developed by Chuck Forsberg in 1986. This improved performance compared to older protocols as well as offered restart able transfers, auto-start by the sender, an expanded 32-bit CRC. The key improvement in ZMODEM was the introduction of sliding window support for improved performance.

Generally file transfer protocols break down a file into a series of *packets*, and then send them one-at-a-time to the receiver. If the packet is received correctly, an acknowledgement message is sent and the sender then starts sending the next packet.

This became popular in 1990s and replaced earlier protocols such as XMODEM and YMODEM.

Zener Diode

The device is named after its discoverer Clarence Zener. This is a special kind of diode which allows current to flow in the forward direction as well as to flow in the reverse direction when the voltage is above a certain value known as the breakdown voltage. The normal diode does not permit to flow the current in reverse direction.

In normal diode when the reverse bias breakdown voltage is exceeded, it subjects to high current due to avalanche breakdown. If this current is not controlled, the diode will burn due to excessive heat. In the case of a large forward bias the diode exhibits a voltage drop due to its junction built-in voltage and internal resistance. The amount of the voltage drop depends on the semiconductor material and the doping concentrations.

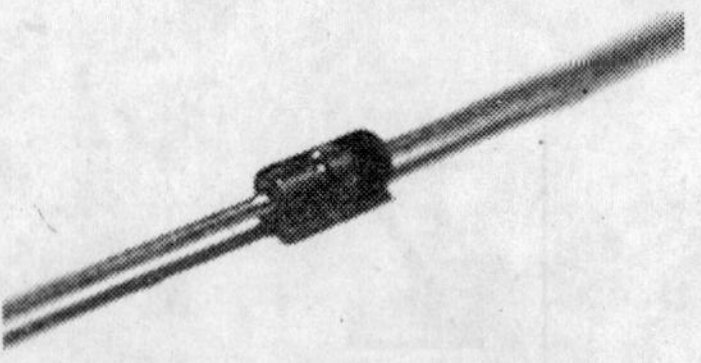

❑❑❑